MY ÁNTONIA

OTHER TITLES IN THE GREENHAVEN PRESS LITERARY COMPANION SERIES:

AMERICAN AUTHORS

Maya Angelou
Stephen Crane
Emily Dickinson
William Faulkner
F. Scott Fitzgerald
Robert Frost
Nathaniel Hawthorne
Ernest Hemingway
Arthur Miller
Flannery O'Connor
Eugene O'Neill
Edgar Allan Poe
John Steinbeck
Mark Twain
Walt Whitman
Thornton Wilder

AMERICAN LITERATURE

The Adventures of
  Huckleberry Finn
The Adventures of Tom
  Sawyer
Black Boy
The Call of the Wild
The Catcher in the Rye
The Crucible
Death of a Salesman
Ethan Frome
Fahrenheit 451
A Farewell to Arms
The Glass Menagerie
The Grapes of Wrath
The Great Gatsby
Native Son
Of Mice and Men
The Old Man and the Sea
One Flew Over the Cuckoo's
  Nest
Our Town
The Pearl
A Raisin in the Sun
The Red Pony
The Scarlet Letter
A Separate Peace
To Kill a Mockingbird
Twelve Angry Men

THE GREENHAVEN PRESS
Literary Companion
TO AMERICAN LITERATURE

READINGS ON

MY ÁNTONIA

Christopher Smith, *Book Editor*

David L. Bender, *Publisher*
Bruno Leone, *Executive Editor*
Bonnie Szumski, *Series Editor*

Greenhaven Press, Inc., San Diego, CA

Every effort has been made to trace the owners of copyrighted material. The articles in this volume may have been edited for content, length, and/or reading level. The titles have been changed to enhance the editorial purpose. Those interested in locating the original source will find the complete citation on the first page of each article.

Library of Congress Cataloging-in-Publication Data

Readings on My Ántonia / Christopher Smith, book editor.
        p.   cm. — (The Greenhaven Press literary
    companion to American literature)
    Includes bibliographical references and index.
    ISBN 0-7377-0180-3 (pbk. : alk. paper) —
ISBN 0-7377-0181-1 (lib. bdg. : alk. paper)
    1. Cather, Willa, 1873–1947. My Ántonia. 2. Frontier
and pioneer life in literature. 3. Women pioneers in
literature. 4. Nebraska—In literature. I. Title: My Ántonia.
II. Smith, Christopher, 1963–   III. Series.

PS3505.A87 M89457   2001
813'.52—dc21   00-064614

Cover photo: © Bettmann/Corbis
Library of Congress, 17

Copyright © 2001 by Greenhaven Press, Inc.
PO Box 289009
San Diego, CA 92198-9009
Printed in the U.S.A.

> *One of the people who interested me most as a child was the Bohemian hired girl of one of our neighbors, who was so good to me. She was one of the truest artists I ever knew in the keenness and sensitiveness of her enjoyment, in her love of people and in her willingness to take pains. I did not realize all this as a child, but Annie fascinated me, and I always had it in mind to write a story about her.*

—Willa Cather, remembering
Annie Pavelka, her inspiration
for Ántonia Shimerda

CONTENTS

that this past can never be recovered or lived again makes *My Ántonia* a classic "American pastoral."

Chapter 3: Character and Character Foils in *My Ántonia*

The quest for success in terms of wealth, the approval of the community, and a more elusive state of contentment is a persistent feature of the lives of the major characters in *My Ántonia.*

Chapter 4: Critical Debates over *My Ántonia*

FOREWORD

"'Tis the good reader that
makes the good book."

Ralph Waldo Emerson

The story's bare facts are simple: The captain, an old and scarred seafarer, walks with a peg leg made of whale ivory. He relentlessly drives his crew to hunt the world's oceans for the great white whale that crippled him. After a long search, the ship encounters the whale and a fierce battle ensues. Finally the captain drives his harpoon into the whale, but the harpoon line catches the captain about the neck and drags him to his death.

A simple story, a straightforward plot—yet, since the 1851 publication of Herman Melville's *Moby-Dick*, readers and critics have found many meanings in the struggle between Captain Ahab and the whale. To some, the novel is a cautionary tale that depicts how Ahab's obsession with revenge leads to his insanity and death. Others believe that the whale represents the unknowable secrets of the universe and that Ahab is a tragic hero who dares to challenge fate by attempting to discover this knowledge. Perhaps Melville intended Ahab as a criticism of Americans' tendency to become involved in well-intentioned but irrational causes. Or did Melville model Ahab after himself, letting his fictional character express his anger at what he perceived as a cruel and distant god?

Although literary critics disagree over the meaning of *Moby-Dick*, readers do not need to choose one particular interpretation in order to gain an understanding of Melville's novel. Instead, by examining various analyses, they can gain numerous insights into the issues that lie under the surface of the basic plot. Studying the writings of literary critics can also aid readers in making their own assessments of *Moby-Dick* and other literary works and in developing analytical thinking skills.

The Greenhaven Literary Companion Series was created with these goals in mind. Designed for young adults, this unique anthology series provides an engaging and comprehensive introduction to literary analysis and criticism. The essays included in the Literary Companion Series are chosen for their accessibility to a young adult audience and are expertly edited in consideration of both the reading and comprehension levels of this audience. In addition, each essay is introduced by a concise summation that presents the contributing writer's main themes and insights. Every anthology in the Literary Companion Series contains a varied selection of critical essays that cover a wide time span and express diverse views. Wherever possible, primary sources are represented through excerpts from authors' notebooks, letters, and journals and through contemporary criticism.

Each title in the Literary Companion Series pays careful consideration to the historical context of the particular author or literary work. In-depth biographies and detailed chronologies reveal important aspects of authors' lives and emphasize the historical events and social milieu that influenced their writings. To facilitate further research, every anthology includes primary and secondary source bibliographies of articles and/or books selected for their suitability for young adults. These engaging features make the Greenhaven Literary Companion series ideal for introducing students to literary analysis in the classroom or as a library resource for young adults researching the world's great authors and literature.

Exceptional in its focus on young adults, the Greenhaven Literary Companion Series strives to present literary criticism in a compelling and accessible format. Every title in the series is intended to spark readers' interest in leading American and world authors, to help them broaden their understanding of literature, and to encourage them to formulate their own analyses of the literary works that they read. It is the editors' hope that young adult readers will find these anthologies to be true companions in their study of literature.

INTRODUCTION

In one of *My Ántonia*'s most memorable scenes, the novel's narrator, Jim Burden, marvels at the simple beauty of an old plough silhouetted against the backdrop of the sun as it sets on the prairie. To Jim, this unremarkable farming implement comes to embody something more, and is magnified in his imagination into a monument "heroic in size, a picture writing on the sun." This scene manages to encapsulate the artistry and continuing appeal of *My Ántonia*. Out of the simplest of elements, Willa Cather managed to construct a narrative that imbued the ordinary with an epic significance. In the 1890s, regionalist writers had begun to chronicle the lives of midwestern American farmers and the small towns that dotted the immense landscape. However, until Willa Cather began drawing on her childhood memories of Nebraska, no one had come so close to conveying the spirit of the land or the humanity of the people who struggled to fashion a living from it. *My Ántonia* transformed a small farming community into a testament to the pioneer spirit and the growing power of America, and readers have consistently responded to its appeal. Cather felt that with *My Ántonia* she had made a true and lasting contribution to American literature, and on the whole critics and readers continue to agree with her. Immediately recognized as a novel of unique beauty, power, and significance upon its publication in 1918, *My Ántonia* has remained the most successful and immediately recognizable of all Willa Cather's novels.

My Ántonia is narrated in a simple and rather episodic style by Jim Burden, a middle-aged lawyer who looks back on his youth in Black Hawk, Nebraska, as the happiest time of his life. Jim manages to convey the awe and wonder that the harsh, unbroken prairie inspired in all those who came to it, as well as the stoic endurance of the immigrants who eventually created thriving, prosperous farms out of nothing. Through Jim, readers are introduced to Ántonia Shimerda, a

Bohemian girl who comes to embody more than anyone else the vitality of life on the frontier. The struggles and ultimate success of Ántonia, and to a lesser extent the other immigrant girls Jim knew in his youth, form the core of the novel, and to Jim represent the most noble aspirations of frontier settlement in America. Cather's unreserved admiration for the German, Scandinavian, and Bohemian immigrants who came to the midwest in the late nineteenth century was something altogether new and radical at a time when immigrants were either feared or looked down on by native-born Americans.

However, *My Ántonia* would not be the novel it is if it were merely a fond, idealistic recollection of youth. Beneath the novel's apparent simplicity run tensions and contradictions. Jim's presentation of pastoral beauty is often disrupted by scenes of terrible violence and small-town pettiness that serve to remind us that innocence never lasts long and is inevitably corrupted. What emerges, despite Jim's determination to idealize both his past and Ántonia, is an unflinching view of life as a difficult and at times tragic struggle, where happiness is always elusive and difficult to keep once attained. The human quest for a true and lasting sense of contentment was a feature of all of Cather's writing, and she ends her novel by vividly and unforgettably portraying Ántonia's triumph in finding what she truly wants from her life. While *My Ántonia*'s other characters, including Jim, have progressively lost their sense of purpose, Ántonia has defied all the odds and has created the thriving farm and family she knew she always wanted. Through Ántonia, Cather manages to both celebrate the true pioneer spirit and question society's misguided beliefs regarding what one truly needs to be happy.

My Ántonia has received a great deal of attention from critics since its publication, and *Readings on My Ántonia* reflects the broad range of responses the novel has generated. Essays on traditional features such as the novel's setting, characters, and themes are balanced by explorations of its style and vigorous debate over whether the novel is a success. Despite the variety of their focus, all the selections illustrate the enduring power of a novel that continues to have a special place in American literature.

WILLA CATHER: A BIOGRAPHY

No other writer evoked the life and landscape of nineteenth century Nebraska better than Willa Cather; for that reason many readers assume that Nebraska was her birthplace, and that she must have lived there all her life. Cather was in fact born in Back Creek, Virginia, and did not move to Nebraska until she was nearly ten. By the time of Willa's birth on December 7, 1873, the Cathers had been living in this poor farming community, located about fifty miles northwest of Washington, D.C., for nearly one hundred years. The first Cather in America, Jasper, Willa's great-great-grandfather, had been a schoolteacher in western Pennsylvania before he moved to Back Creek Valley after the American Revolution. Her great-grandfather, James Cather, born in 1795, was a respected and admired member of the Back Creek Valley community, later representing the district in the Virginia legislature. James was one of seven children; he married Ann Howard in 1819, and the couple raised eight children, including son William, the grandfather of Willa. William married Caroline in 1846, and both were important figures in Willa Cather's life. Willa's grandparents settled on a large farm a mile east of the village of Back Creek in 1851, and prospered there. Like Jim Burden's grandparents in *My Ántonia*, they would journey westward from Virginia and settle in Nebraska.

Virginia was the cradle of resistance to the North during the Civil War, and like many American families at the time, the Cathers were divided over slavery and whether to support the Union or Confederate cause. Few of Back Creek's struggling farmers owned slaves, and Willa's grandfather William was typical of many in the community in his support for the preservation of the Union and the Northern cause. On the other hand, his father James was a strong believer in state's rights and sided with the Confederacy even though he did not support the institution of slavery. The Civil War was a tense time for Back Creek—families and friends were divided, and both Union and Confederate soldiers often moved through the area, usually looting and stealing from the local farms. At the beginning of the war, Willa's father, Charles, had been too young for military duty, but William Cather later moved his son to West Virginia so that he would not be conscripted into the Confederate army.

The Civil War left the defeated South in desperate circumstances economically and politically, but William Cather was rewarded for his allegiance to the Union by being named sheriff of Frederick County; moreover, the Cather family farm had not suffered major damage during the war. Resentments brewed, but slowly the South began to heal, and sectional arguments over who had supported what cause began to fade. The marriage of Charles Cather, the son of a Unionist, to Mary Virginia Boak, whose three brothers had served in the Confederate army, was emblematic of this communal reconciliation. They were married on December 5, 1872, in the home of the bride's mother, Rachel Boak—a formidable woman who was to play a major role in Willa Cather's life and fiction. To her granddaughter an embodiment of the grace, strength, and dignity of the Old South, Grandmother Boak would serve as the inspiration for Rachel Blake in Cather's last novel, *Sapphira and the Slave Girl* (1940), and for Mrs. Harris in Willa's highly autobiographical short story "Old Mrs. Harris" (1932).

Willa was born almost exactly a year after her parents' marriage, on December 7, 1873. A good farmer and later a competent businessman with some legal training, her father was a gentle and sensitive man. Willa was much closer to him than she was to her mother, a highly competent, energetic, and strong-willed schoolteacher. Charles and Mary Cather would have three more children: Roscoe (born 1877), Douglass (born 1880), and Jessica (born 1881). The Cather-Boak marriage had forged an alliance between two prominent Back Creek families, and Willa was raised in a financially comfortable and secure environment. The relative prosperity the Cathers enjoyed allowed Willa to remember her life in Back Creek as idyllic, characterized by an easy pace and sense of tradition and charm. Time and again, Cather's novels draw on and celebrate the places and people of a vanished past. Cather's emphasis on the past serves in turn to highlight the deficiencies of twentieth-century life, and there is no question that her early exposure to rural life in Virginia exacerbated her nostalgic tendencies and her hostility toward "progress."

THE CATHERS' WESTWARD MIGRATION

In 1877, Willa's grandparents decided to join one of their children, George, who had settled with his wife in Nebraska, and start their own farm. Charles was left in charge of the old family farm in Back Creek, and he managed the property in a competent and orderly manner until 1883. On a visit to Nebraska in 1880, Charles was impressed by the fertility of the land and his parents' and brothers' successful farms. However, reluctant to leave the land his family had inhabited for over a century, three more years passed before he was finally persuaded to join them. By April 1883 Willa's family had arrived in Nebraska. They began a new life in a land that could not possibly have been more different from the rolling hills, dense woods, and cultivated fields of Virginia.

At first glance, it may seem strange that the Cather family should risk leaving a successful, prosperous farm and abandoning their prominent position in an established community. However, the Cathers' westward movement reflected widespread demographic trends in late-nineteenth-century America. The Homestead Act of 1862 offered free land in the territories to anyone prepared to live on it, and the completion of the transcontinental railroad in 1869 made the west accessible. At the same time, railroads created the means by which farm produce could be transported to urban, East Coast markets. To many easterners and immigrants, the West offered irresistible opportunities and embodied the energy and promise of the American nation as it emerged from the trauma of civil war. The family initially settled in Catherton, Nebraska, named by and for Charles's brother George, but Charles Cather farmed the land for less than two years. In 1884 he moved his family to nearby Red Cloud, Nebraska, establishing himself as a realtor and insurance agent. Red Cloud, a thriving market and railroad junction town of about eighteen hundred inhabitants, would be Willa's home for the next six years. The Cathers lived in a pleasant but somewhat cramped frame house close to the town's business district.

When Jim Burden arrives from Virginia at the beginning of *My Ántonia*, he feels a profound sense of loneliness. Noting the landscape's enormity and its lack of apparent variety compared with Virginia, he feels "erased, blotted out." In this instance, Jim Burden is mirroring Cather's initial response to Nebraska and the sense of dislocation its landscape imposed on her consciousness. Cather would remember a sense of intense homesickness, but she was eventually reconciled to the

Nebraska landscape and came to love it more than any other. Another aspect of Nebraska she came to love was the immense and varied immigrant population. Apart from a French Canadian settlement north of Red Cloud, Swedes, Russians, Danes, Norwegians, Bohemians, and Germans had established farms, families, and burgeoning communities in the outlying districts. By 1910, Nebraska's population was 1.2 million, of which 900,000 were of immigrant stock. Cather's fiction reflects a reverence for the struggles and triumphs of the state's immigrants, and disdain for the indifference native-born Americans exhibited toward them. One need only compare the openness and vitality of the immigrant "hired girls" with the mean-spirited and stifling conformity of Black Hawk's burgeoning middle class in *My Ántonia* to see where Cather's sympathies lay. Most importantly for her fiction, Cather would remember spending afternoons with older immigrant women who told stories of their respective European homelands. As a listener, Cather would remember that "I have never felt an excitement more intense than I used to feel when I spent a morning with one of these old women baking or butter-making. I used to ride home in the most unreasonable state of excitement; I always felt . . . as if I had actually got inside another person's skin."

Early Intellectual Growth

Despite its small size and relative isolation on the frontier, Red Cloud was home to a number of cultured and stimulating people, many of whom contributed to Willa Cather's education. Besides her Grandmother Boak, who had moved with the family, there was Miss Eva J. King, a schoolteacher who recognized and encouraged Cather's talents in her early school years. The principal of the high school, Mrs. Goudy, was such a positive influence on Willa Cather that the two remained friends for forty years.

Many of the people Cather knew in Red Cloud would have a different kind of influence on her, ultimately appearing in one form or another in her short stories and novels. For instance, a German couple, Mr. and Mrs. Charles Weiner, had an extensive library that Willa was allowed to borrow from whenever she liked. Nearly fifty years later, they were sympathetically portrayed as the Rosens in "Old Mrs. Harris." Cather also established an important friendship with one of Red Cloud's foremost families, the Miners, the members of which were fictionally transformed into the Harlings in *My*

Ántonia. Evenings in the Miner home offered Willa her first exposure to classical music and opera, and set in motion a passion that would stay with her the rest of her life. The Miner daughters—Mary, Carrie, and Irene—were Cather's closest childhood companions and remained lifelong friends. Significantly, a young Bohemian woman who worked for the Miners, Annie Sadilek (later Pavelka), would some thirty years later serve as the inspiration for perhaps Cather's most memorable character—Ántonia Shimerda.

Cather was also a frequent visitor to her Uncle George's farm, and there were many picnics and outings around the immediate countryside. During her years in Red Cloud, fictional characters began to take shape in her imagination, and Red Cloud's inhabitants served as her primary source of inspiration. Just as importantly, Cather also absorbed the dramatic moods and seasons of the Nebraska landscape, and she would return to these memories time and again in her best fiction.

Willa Cather

Outside of school, Willa began to read deeply and extensively in European literature. Besides the classics and Shakespeare, she knew and loved the work of many of the great nineteenth-century novelists—Dickens, Sir Walter Scott, Thackeray, Poe, and Hawthorne. She had a special affection for the French writer Alexandre Dumas, author of *The Count of Monte Cristo*, and the Russian novelist Leo Tolstoy, whose epic descriptions of his land and the towering passions of his characters thrilled her.

By all accounts, the young Willa Cather was a gifted, precocious child who managed to draw a great deal of attention from adults during her Red Cloud days. Besides her gregarious and sociable nature (which she would suppress in favor of a need for anonymity and privacy as her fame grew), Cather also developed some rather unique tastes regarding her appearance. Against all prevailing fashions, she had her hair cut very short, would usually sign her name "William Cather," and refused to wear skirts and dresses, preferring boy's clothes. From an early age, it was obvious that she had no intention of becoming the kind of pampered middle-class parlor girl proficient in the domestic arts of cooking and sewing that society's code of conformity expected of her.

Cather found her chief creative outlet at this time in drama. With her friends she performed many extemporaneous "skits" and more formalized amateur theatrical productions. Local newspaper reviews from the 1880s covered Willa Cather's performances, calling attention to her impressive powers of elocution, and there is a photo of her in a performance of *Beauty and the Beast*, which she performed with the Miner children in 1888. Besides her involvement in drama and the large amounts of time she devoted to studying the classics and reading novels, Cather also found the time to report the local high school news for the *Red Cloud Argus*. Like Jim Burden in *My Ántonia*, she delivered an impressive speech at her high school graduation in June 1890. She was sixteen and a half, and ready to enroll at the University of Nebraska in Lincoln.

CATHER'S UNIVERSITY DAYS

Willa Cather arrived in Lincoln, the state capital, in September 1890; although Lincoln's population was only thirty-five thousand, the move was a dramatic change for a young woman from a rough frontier town. Lincoln was a bustling and thriving commercial center, inhabited by educated professionals as well as more dubious western speculators and opportunists. Because it was a major railroad center, the very best theatrical and musical companies would stop there on their way farther west to Denver and San Francisco. If Cather's reading and penchant for drama began in Red Cloud, her much broader exposure to first-class performance art in Lincoln initiated her early career as a reviewer and cemented her lifelong love of music and drama.

In 1890, the University of Nebraska enrolled somewhere between three and four hundred students, but like the state itself it was growing rapidly. By the time Cather graduated, enrollment stood at nine hundred. Although the university was still relatively young and raw, it employed many fine, committed teachers. The sheer variety of students, coming from all corners of the state, made for a stimulating environment. Cather was not immediately admitted into the freshman class, since the Red Cloud High School curriculum did not meet all the stringent requirements of the university. She therefore attended classes at the university's preparatory school, and after a year she was allowed to enroll as a freshman.

Both her professors and fellow students remembered Cather

as bright, diligent, and ambitious. Cather's initial intention had been to study medicine, but her love of literature and the classics soon asserted itself, and she switched to humanities. An indication of her distinction as a student came in 1891, when she wrote a class assignment on British philosopher Thomas Carlyle that so impressed her professor he had it published in the *Nebraska State Journal*—a remarkable achievement for a girl of seventeen. Cather remained an outstanding student though she had to work virtually full time as a journalist in her junior and senior years to put herself through college. A severe recession struck Nebraska and the entire country in 1893, and her father was suddenly hard pressed to support the family, let alone pay for his daughter's board and tuition.

As in Red Cloud, her somewhat eccentric and highly individual personality asserted itself. Cather was always an opinionated, polarizing figure who rarely suffered fools gladly. With the exception of Herbert Bates, who recognized and encouraged her writing talent, Cather found her professors uninspiring and rather pompous, and she did not hesitate to communicate these feelings to the professors themselves. Many of her early reviews are memorable for the extent to which they savaged productions she did not like, and she was either ardently admired or utterly detested by students and professors. Creative writing and an intense appreciation of art and music increasingly became the means by which Cather found fulfillment and defined the path her life would take. From this point on, her goal in life was to write books and live the kind of life that would allow her to write without interruption. Forced to support herself, however, she was not entirely free to write fiction, and for the next twenty years she had to settle for a pattern that developed in college—that of maintaining a balance between her creative impulses and the need to make a living as a reviewer and editor.

THE BEGINNINGS OF A CAREER IN JOURNALISM

On November 5, 1893, Cather began contributing a regular column—"One Way of Putting It"—to the *Nebraska State Journal*. She was paid one dollar per thousand-word column. From these humble beginnings, Cather would some fifteen years later reach the top of the journalistic profession as the managing editor of *McClure's*, one of America's best-selling magazines. The years 1894 and 1895 were hectic, since she had to submit enough articles and reviews to the *Journal* to support herself as well as manage full-time studies. It was a rewarding kind of double life. In her senior year, Cather published ninety-five newspaper articles and reviews, which helped immeasurably in developing her skills as a critic, journalist, and fiction writer. She also managed to meet such famous figures as the short-story writer, novelist, and newspaperman Stephen Crane and Populist politician William Jennings Bryan. By the time she graduated on June 12, 1895, with a bachelor of arts degree, she had an abundance of experience that would serve her well in the future.

After graduation, Cather continued submitting reviews for the *Journal* and briefly secured a job at the *Courier*, a weekly paper that covered the arts and society in Lincoln. She applied for a position as instructor of English at the university, but she was turned down, largely because the head of the English department disliked her intensely. For the next year, Cather divided her time between Lincoln and Red Cloud, piecing together a living by writing reviews, but she was unable to secure a full-time position as either a teacher or journalist. As far as her own writing was concerned, though, she achieved something of a breakthrough when her short story, "On the Divide," was published in a prominent national magazine. The story is written in the bleak manner of regionalist writer Hamlin Garland, and Cather would later disown it, but there is no question that it gave her confidence at a time when she believed her career plans had stalled. Meanwhile, her reviews praised the romantic impulse in literature at the expense of the realist movement led by William Dean Howells. Cather's ideal—and an influence she would later have to discard in order to find her own voice—was Henry James, whom she saw as possessing "the foremost mind that ever applied itself to literature in America." Perhaps James appealed to Cather because he, too, was a worshiper of art for art's sake, and was prepared to sacrifice much to realize artistic perfection in his own work.

RELOCATION TO PITTSBURGH

In the spring of 1896, Cather was offered a position as editor of *Home Monthly* magazine, a Pittsburgh, Pennsylvania, publication aimed at America's enormous female readership. Cather was offered the job through the efforts of George Gerwig, a friend of hers from Lincoln who had relocated to Pittsburgh. It was a tremendous break since she was desperate to move out of Red Cloud and establish herself in a profession. Not surprisingly, she jumped at the opportunity, and arrived in Pittsburgh in late June.

Pittsburgh in 1896 was the center of the steel industry in America, and the industrialist giant dominating this immense productive enterprise was Andrew Carnegie, one of the great "robber baron" millionaires of the post–Civil War era. Thanks to Carnegie's largesse, Pittsburgh had a magnificent auditorium, library, and art museum, and Cather reveled in the many cultural opportunities this bustling city of four hundred thousand offered. Exercising almost complete editorial control over *Home Monthly*, she often, over the next year, contributed her own material, eventually publishing nine stories. By all accounts she was a diligent, versatile, and inventive editor, and often, combining her editorials and book columns with her fictional contributions, over half the magazine came from Cather's prolific pen. She also lost no time in making the most of her love for opera and drama by writing reviews and criticism part time for the *Pittsburgh Leader*, the city's largest newspaper.

Although her work kept her busy, Cather made friends easily and managed to have a busy social life. She is known to have received and turned down two marriage proposals, but like Lena Lingard in *My Ántonia*, Cather was too fond of her independence and too dedicated to her own ambitions to accept the compromises of marriage. Her indifference, if not hostility, to marriage is found throughout her fiction, where married men and women are often unhappy and oppressed by their circumstances. Cather's only true love and partner throughout life was art, and the pursuit of truth and beauty in her fiction. Her novels and short stories repeatedly illustrate her belief that art and domesticity do not mix. Cather's early heroines, such as Alexandra Bergson in *O Pioneers!* (1913), and Thea Kronberg in *The Song of the Lark* (1915), do eventually marry, but only after their most ardent passions and goals in life have been fulfilled, and after their achievements cannot be diminished through marriage.

In July 1897, only a year after she took the job, Cather severed her connection with the *Home Monthly*, and accepted a better-paid, more demanding position at the *Pittsburgh Leader* as a telegraph editor, responsible for cutting or expanding foreign cables for each day's final edition. She continued her remarkable output of reviews and articles in her spare time, and often sent columns back to Nebraska. Socially Cather developed an important friendship with musician and composer Ethelbert Nevin, whose creativity and dedication to his craft matched her idea of how a true artist should live his life.

Cather's most important Pittsburgh friend, though, was undoubtedly Isabelle McClung, whom she met in 1899. The daughter of a distinguished Pittsburgh judge, the two were inseparable for the rest of Cather's time in Pittsburgh, saw a great deal of each other after Cather moved to New York in 1906, and remained lifelong friends. McClung took a deep interest in Cather's evolving career as a writer, but biographers have focused most of their speculation on the intimacy of their relationship. Little evidence indicates the nature of their bond because Cather destroyed all their correspondence when McClung died in 1936. There is, however, no doubt that Cather's love for McClung induced her to stay in Pittsburgh after she tired of daily journalism and resigned her position at the *Leader* in 1900—the same year she moved into the McClung household.

Also in 1900 Cather, having momentarily tired of journalism, took a position at Central High School, teaching English composition and Latin. She would remain there for three years before moving to Allegheny High School, where she taught until 1906. Cather's students remembered her as a dedicated and rigorous teacher who rewarded talent and excellence but who was not above belittling students who produced substandard work. On the whole Cather enjoyed teaching; she maintained many years later that she would have been happy to remain in the profession, since the money was good and she enjoyed having the summers off to concentrate on her writing.

Cather's salary, and the fact that she saved a lot of money by living with the McClungs, allowed her to travel to Europe for the first time in 1902. For a young woman who had grown up reading the novels, seeing the drama, and hearing the music of nineteenth-century Europe, actually visiting England and France was truly exhilarating. Biographer Sharon O'Brien notes that, in the tradition of American novelists Nathaniel Hawthorne and Henry James, Cather also saw herself as "the American writer embarking on a journey to discover her origins, to confront history and the past." Together Cather and McClung spent most of their time visiting literary and artistic landmarks. Although Cather returned to Europe on a number of occasions later in her life, it was this first visit that she remembered most intensely.

A VOLUME OF POETRY AND A COLLECTION OF SHORT STORIES

Many Cather devotees are surprised that her first publication was a small volume of poetry. Yet in the late 1890s and early

1900s, Cather was working full time as either a teacher or journalist, and poetry served as a quick and efficient means of setting an idea down on paper and carrying that idea through to its completion. A novel, on the other hand, demanded concentrated periods of time, which Cather at this point in her life did not have. *April Twilights* came out in 1903; Cather, realizing she was a competent but not a great poet, would later regret that she published it at all. Although the poems lyrically evoke nostalgia for the myths and glories of a better, simpler world in much the same manner as her later novels would, Cather never seriously tried her hand at poetry again. Around 1900, Cather had prophetically written that America needed a writer who would evoke and celebrate "the people on whom the burden of labor rested, who plant the corn and cut the wheat and drive the drays and mine the coal and forge the iron and move the world." She was in effect outlining her great theme, but she had not yet managed to transform this theme into art, and Nebraska barely appears in *April Twilights*.

The collection was nevertheless a promising beginning. Around this time Cather met the famous magazine publisher S.S. McClure, whose *McClure's Magazine* was at the time one of the best-selling and most celebrated magazines in America. Will Owen Jones, a journalism colleague from Lincoln, had recommended Cather's stories to McClure's talent-scouting cousin, and out of the blue Cather was invited to New York for an interview. McClure, impressed by her work, offered to publish her stories in book form, and wanted his magazine to have first refusal on all future work. For Cather, this was a dizzying sequence of events, and the first consequence of her meeting with McClure was the publication of a collection of her short stories, *The Troll Garden*, in 1905. Detailing the sacrifices, joys, and sorrows that attend those who pursue truth in art, this collection clearly showed Cather's undeniable talents, and included some of her best-known short stories, such as "A Death in the Desert," "The Sculptor's Funeral," and "Paul's Case."

AN OFFER OF EMPLOYMENT IN NEW YORK

In the spring of 1906, McClure was in desperate need of a managing editor for his magazine, and knowing Cather's journalistic experience and abilities, he made her an offer so generous that she could not refuse. *McClure's Magazine* was at this time the most prestigious (or most notorious, depending on one's point of view) "muckraking" magazine in America. Muckraking journalism was committed to exposing the corruption and greed of corporations and government at all levels. It was in *McClure's* that Ida Tarbell published her famous exposé of Standard Oil's monopolistic practices, and Lincoln Steffens outlined the criminal graft practiced by local government officials in Minneapolis. Aside from these sensational articles, which led to important reforms in American society, *McClure's* also published some of the best fiction of the best writers in America and England. The work of Rudyard Kipling, Joseph Conrad, Robert Louis Stevenson, Jack London, and Mark Twain graced the magazine's pages. Cather had suddenly gone from being an obscure high school teacher and part-time publisher of poems and short stories to a position as editor of the most influential magazine in America.

Conservative and apolitical, Cather was not particularly interested in the magazine's reform impulses. However, she tackled the literary submissions with zeal, as she did New York—the city that would remain her home for the rest of her life. Just as Lincoln had been a cultural leap for her after Red Cloud, and Pittsburgh a further expansion of opportunities, New York catered to her every musical, dramatic, and literary need.

By her midthirties, Willa Cather had carved out a staggeringly successful career for herself in a man's world, but at the cost of putting her own writing career on hold. The number of stories Cather either published or wrote declined dramatically from 1907 to 1911, partly because McClure contractually obliged her to complete research already begun by the magazine and write a biography of Mary Baker G. Eddy, the founder of the Christian Science movement. Although these constraints were frustrating, Cather was very loyal to McClure and knew how much she owed him for the opportunities he had given her.

Cather's work at *McClure's* allowed her to meet many influential people and travel widely. In 1908, while researching the book on Mary Baker G. Eddy in Boston, she met Ferris Greenslet, an editor at Houghton Mifflin who became a lifelong friend. Although Cather would later leave Greenslet's firm for the publishing house of Alfred A. Knopf, Houghton Mifflin would publish Cather's first four novels. In Boston, Cather also met Sarah Orne Jewett, an important New England regionalist writer. Jewett would have such an important influence on Cather's choice of Nebraska as the best possible subject and setting for her fiction that five years later Cather would dedicate her breakthrough novel, *O Pioneers!*, to Jewett. Writers such as Zoe Adkins and Elizabeth Sergeant also became important friends, and Sergeant later wrote an influential memoir of their friendship after Cather died.

McClure rewarded Cather for her work with a four-month trip to Italy in 1908, which she took with Isabelle McClung. A year later she went to England in search of new writing talent for the magazine. When Cather returned from Italy, she moved into an apartment with Edith Lewis, another Nebraskan who had moved to New York to work in the publishing business. Cather had known Lewis in Lincoln, and helped find her a position at *McClure's* as a proofreader. The two would live together for the next forty years, until Cather's death in 1947; after Isabelle McClung, this was the closest and most important friendship of Cather's life.

ALEXANDER'S BRIDGE AND A CAREER AS A FULL-TIME NOVELIST

In September 1911, Cather asked for a six-month leave of absence from *McClure's* to rest and concentrate on her writing. When she returned to find McClure himself had been effectively removed from his position of authority with the magazine, she chose to become a freelance contributor. Leaving such a prestigious and well-paid position at *McClure's* for a much more uncertain career as a professional novelist and freelance writer took a great deal of courage, but in 1912 Cather's confidence was strengthened by the publication of *Alexander's Bridge*, which she had managed to write while working full time at *McClure's*.

Alexander's Bridge (1912) was loosely based on a true story, the collapse of a bridge near Quebec in 1907 that killed more than eighty men, including the chief engineer. The novel's main character, Bartley Alexander, a middle-aged, successful engineer, is the first of what would become a stock character in Cather's fiction: the outwardly successful but inwardly troubled and dissatisfied male. One only need look at the duality of *My Ántonia*'s Jim Burden to see how Cather successfully integrated this figure into the fabric of her fiction. Bartley Alexander is essentially an artist and a romantic; as the novel develops he increasingly feels he has sacrificed his artistic impulses in the name of public success. A failing marriage and a revived affair from his student days increase his self-doubt, and his death on the bridge—supposedly his greatest public triumph––finally puts to rest an agonized soul. *Alexander's Bridge* did not sell particularly well, but it received encouraging reviews. Yet by this time Cather had already moved on, and had published in *McClure's* a short story that would set the tone for her next novel, *O Pioneers!* (1913).

WILLA CATHER'S TRUE SUBJECT

The story Cather published was called "The Bohemian Girl," and it was important to Cather not only because Nebraska was its setting but also because in it she began to see the drama of the immigrant experience on the plains as the richest feature of Nebraska life. Though Cather liked the story when it came out, she would later realize that it served only as a springboard for *O Pioneers!* "The Bohemian Girl" shared an important theme in *O Pioneers!:* the virtuous simplicity of subsistence farming in conflict with a new faith in materialism, and the extent to which this conflict can destroy a family. The story was a first step in an important process whereby Cather brought the Nebraska of her childhood to the forefront of her imagination and learned to use it dispassionately. As she would later acknowledge to an interviewer regarding the success of her Nebraska novels, "When I began to remember, I began to write."

O Pioneers! began as two separate short stories, "Alexandra" and "The White Mulberry Tree." The first introduced Alexandra Bergson, the character who would become the novel's heroine; the second dealt with an adulterous affair violently avenged by the wronged husband. In an exhilarating moment of artistic clarity, Cather was able to bring the two stories together and create the main body of the novel. Yet she was also able to infuse *O Pioneers!* with a sense of mythic heroism. Above and beyond the dramas and tragedies of the Bergson family, is the monumental struggle to settle the land, and the unending hardships the settlers must prevail over. As in *My Ántonia*, the land is a character in itself, defining the lives of the people who inhabit it, and both giving and withholding its rewards. The reviews that followed the publication of *O Pioneers!* were uniformly positive. Reviewers and readers alike realized that Cather had brought a significant, even heroic dimension of American history to the forefront of the public imagination, and that she had infused it with visionary and inspiring poetry.

Cather's next novel, *The Song of the Lark* (1915), returned to her earlier preoccupation with art and artists. The novel's heroine is Thea Kronberg, inspired by Olive Fremstad, a Swedish-born immigrant from Minnesota who became a world-renowned opera singer. Central to *The Song of the Lark* is the growth of the artist, the hard sacrifices necessary to fulfill one's artistic potential, and the fact that those destined to be artists can never be satisfied with doing anything else in life. When Cather interviewed Fremstad for an article in *McClure's*, she immediately sympathized with Fremstad's midwestern background, which was so similar to her own. Cather believed that Fremstad had all the toughness and defiance of the pioneer women who settled the frontier, and although there seems to be a huge gulf between Thea Kronberg and Alexandra Bergson, the heroine of *O Pioneers!*, the two are in fact very similar. Like Thea Kronberg, Alexandra Bergson possesses the creative imagination and drive necessary to realize her individual ambitions, though her vision involves building a prosperous farm rather than becoming an opera singer. Both characters are artists in their own right, although Alexandra's claim to this title is less obvious than that of Thea Kronberg. With Alexandra and Thea, Cather had also comfortably settled into a pattern of creating strong-willed female characters, whose courage and strength of character enable them to transcend the roles of wife and mother by which society characteristically defined women.

During the composition of *The Song of the Lark*, Cather continued to contribute to *McClure's*, although she was now able to do so on her terms, and at a more relaxed pace. As a favor to McClure, she agreed to ghost write his autobiography, which came out in 1914. *The Song of the Lark* sold respectably and was generally well received, but later Cather would be critical of the work, maintaining that it was overly long and lacking in structure. In the 1930s, when a collected edition of her novels was being prepared, she would cut over seven thousand words from the novel. Modest royalties from *The Song of the Lark* meant Cather had to continue writing short stories, though she wanted to concentrate entirely on novels. Many of the stories she published at this time were competent but not of the quality of her novels.

Other events in her life were distracting her, leading her to put off beginning a new novel altogether. In November 1915, her friend Isabelle McClung's father died. With Judge McClung's death, the family house, where Cather had composed many stories and lived some of the happiest days of her adult life, was sold. A few months later, Isabelle announced her engagement to a concert violinist, Jan Hambourg. In the space of less than a year, an important chapter in Cather's life had come to a close, and her ties to Pittsburgh had suddenly ended. Due in no small part to these important changes, Cather produced very little work in 1916. However, she revisited New Mexico—an area she had fallen in love with when she first visited in 1908, which she featured in *The Song of the Lark*, and which would become more and more important to her fiction. In the summer and fall she also returned to Red Cloud, and reacquainted herself with Annie Pavelka. It is highly likely that Jim's visit to Ántonia and her family in the final section of *My Ántonia* was based on Cather's own visit to the Pavelka farm in 1916.

MY ÁNTONIA, ONE OF OURS, AND A PULITZER PRIZE

The writing of *My Ántonia* proceeded slowly, mostly because Cather's ongoing need for income meant she had to take time off from the novel to write short stories. Cather wrote *My Ántonia*'s second section, "The Hired Girls," in Jaffrey, New Hampshire, a small town near Mount Monadnock, to which she often returned for the rest of her life. She had promised her publisher that the novel would be ready by November 1917, but she did not complete it until mid-1918. A novel shaped by Cather's own recollections of Red Cloud and the area's immigrant farmers, *My Ántonia* is a drama of memory. It reflects the continuation of a trend in Cather's fiction, first suggested in *O Pioneers!*, that is, the presentation of the past as more appealing than the present. Like Cather, *My Ántonia*'s narrator, Jim Burden, looks back with nostalgia to a simpler time made more real by the struggles of the settlers to wrest a living from the soil; to him, Ántonia Shimerda embodies the best qualities of these settlers. The novel has a noble simplicity that manages to infuse the life of an ordinary immigrant woman with the quality of an enduring myth. Although some reviewers questioned the novel's loosely episodic plot, the consensus was that Cather had broken through to a new level of artistry, and that her fourth novel marked the discovery of her true voice as a writer.

The year 1918 also marked the end of World War I. Like most of her generation, Cather saw the war's widespread carnage as an almost criminal waste of Western civilization's youth. She also shared with other writers the perception that the war had forever changed the world, and due to circumstances in her family she perceived this change in personal as well as more abstract terms. On May 23, 1918, Lieutenant George P. Cather, son of her Uncle George and Aunt Franc, had been killed in action in France. For the next three years, Cather meditated deeply on her cousin as she wrote *One of Ours* (1922). The novel is about an inarticulate young Nebraska man who, when the war comes, leaps at the chance of escaping the only environment he has ever known to seek adventure and glory.

The completion of *One of Ours* was interrupted by an important decision on Cather's part. Since the publication of *The Song of the Lark*, she had become increasingly discontented with her publishing house, Houghton Mifflin, and inclined to seek a publisher who would present and market her work more carefully. Yet due to her friendship with Ferris Greenslet, her editor at Houghton Mifflin, Cather felt a sense of loyalty and was loath to leave. After the publication of *My Ántonia*, though, she was aggressively courted by Alfred A. Knopf, a relative newcomer to the publishing industry who recognized Cather's literary promise. Knopf shrewdly offered to republish Cather's early collection of short stories from 1905, *The Troll Garden*, which Houghton Mifflin had declined to buy the rights to. Knopf's plan turned out better than he hoped, since Cather eagerly accepted his proposal, and then decided to add four recent stories to what she felt were the four best from *The Troll Garden*. The end result, *Youth and the Bright Medusa* (1920), continued Cather's obsession with portraying artists and musicians, and due to Knopf's skillful marketing, it sold very well and earned Cather enough income to devote herself entirely to *One of Ours*. The next year Cather signed with Knopf, beginning a warm, mutually beneficial relationship that thrived until Cather's death twenty-six years later.

Cather had no problem writing the early parts of *One of Ours*, since they were set in Nebraska. However, she felt that if she was going to maintain the novel's level of realism she needed to visit the battlefields of France, where a great deal of the novel's action took place, and she and Edith Lewis left New York in May 1920. Less than two years after the war, France was still in turmoil. However, Cather managed to visit her cousin's grave and tried to acquire the kind of feel for the country necessary to complete the book. She traveled through the south of France, meeting Isabelle Hambourg and her husband, and did not return to New York until mid-

November. *One of Ours* was finally published in September 1922, four years after *My Ántonia.* Cather had struggled a great deal with the novel, and had been impeded by some minor but irritating health problems. The novel itself received mixed reviews, mostly because expectations had been so high after *My Ántonia.* Nevertheless, Cather had again succeeded in creating a complete and richly complex character—Claude Wheeler—who fully engaged readers' sympathies. The weakness of the novel lay in the fact that, despite her research in France, in her war scenes Cather could not match the superb depictions of life in Nebraska that begin the novel. These shortcomings aside, the book sold about fifty-five thousand copies in its first year, and stimulated sales of Cather's other novels. She would never have to worry about money again, and in 1923, *One of Ours* was awarded the Pulitzer Prize.

1923–1928: CATHER'S MIRACULOUS YEARS

Enjoying both financial independence and the unconditional support of her publisher, Cather settled into a comfortable life in New York City with Edith Lewis, punctuated by visits to Grand Manan (an island near New Brunswick, Canada), New Hampshire, Nebraska, and New Mexico. She also published four undisputed masterpieces over the next five years. The three novels she wrote between 1923 and 1928 were *A Lost Lady* (1923), *The Professor's House* (1925), and *Death Comes for the Archbishop* (1927). She also wrote a novella, *My Mortal Enemy* (1926). Together these works placed her in the vanguard of American literature.

The first, *A Lost Lady* (1923), is a short but technically flawless novel that charts the rise and fall of Marian Forrester, as seen through the eyes of a young admirer, Niel Herbert. Cather once again returned to her Red Cloud days to write her best fiction. Marian Forrester is based on Lyra Garber, the wife of a banker and former governor of Nebraska. The couple used to lavishly entertain the railroad magnates who traveled through Red Cloud during Cather's youth, but they eventually lost much of their fortune when Silas's bank failed. In Marian Forrester, Cather created a beautiful, vivacious woman who compromises herself morally by having affairs. Yet she has the strength of character to continue in the face of adversity and successfully remarry after her husband dies and leaves her financially destitute. In choosing to use a male subject to tell the story of a woman, Cather was returning to the narrative technique she employed in *My Ántonia.* Like Jim Burden's misguided disappointments in Ántonia when she does not conform to his expectations, Niel Herbert places Marian Forrester on a pedestal and judges her harshly when she falls short of his unrealistic ideals. Yet both Ántonia and Marian Forrester know what they want from life, and through their strength of character they live rich, successful lives. Cather obviously reveled in creating strong, purposeful females who are misunderstood by the men who tell their stories.

In a 1922 essay titled "The Novel Démeublé," Cather had complained that realist novels had become overfurnished with irrelevant details. She maintained that writers needed to pare down their descriptive passages, leaving only the most essential components so that universal truths might shine through. In the lean yet lyrical economy of *A Lost Lady,* everything Cather includes matters, and there is not a single wasted word, a brilliant embodiment of her theories.

A sign of Cather's growing popularity was that she accepted a Warner Brothers offer for the film rights to *A Lost Lady* for the then-impressive sum of $10,000. Film versions of the novel were made in 1925 and 1934, but Cather never liked cinema or any tampering with her work, and in her will she unequivocally prohibited any future film versions of her novels.

Cather settled into writing her next novel, *The Professor's House,* in 1923, after returning to New York from seven months abroad in Europe. *The Professor's House* returns to the territory of her first novel, *Alexander's Bridge*—to a male figure who has after a long struggle achieved public renown, yet feels he has lost the vital essence of life in the process. Godfrey St. Peter, a professor at a midwestern college, has after many years of sacrifice published a monumental history of the early Spanish explorers in America. Yet St. Peter is also experiencing something of a midlife crisis, and Cather goes on to illustrate how success and money are no guarantee of happiness, and a savage indictment of twentieth-century materialism follows.

My Mortal Enemy, a novella published in 1926, is also a rather bleak work, documenting marital disintegration and the slow decline of a couple's fortunes in life. Critics have noted that *The Professor's House* and *My Mortal Enemy* constitute Cather's most pessimistic work, and that they reflect her disenchantment and contempt for what she saw as the misguided and slavishly materialistic values that dominated American life in the 1920s. From this point on, she increasingly turned to the past in an attempt to illuminate what for her was most admirable about humanity.

Early in his narration of *My Ántonia*, Jim Burden defines happiness as becoming a part of a larger design and being "dissolved into something complete and great." Ántonia Shimerda gives her entire self to the land and her family, and for Jim she represents all that was pure and good about pioneer settlement on the frontier. Cather would return to the idea that true greatness involves a humble and complete dedication to something greater than oneself in *Death Comes for the Archbishop* (1927), which, next to *My Ántonia*, is perhaps her best-loved novel. *Death Comes for the Archbishop* is based on William J. Howlett's *The Life of the Right Reverend Joseph P. Marchebeuf*, which Cather had fortuitously discovered during her visit to New Mexico in 1924. Cather's novelistic treatment of Marchebeuf and Archbishop Jean Baptiste Lamy episodically details their heroic self-sacrifice, piety, and devotion as they reestablish the Catholic faith in the nineteenth-century American Southwest. Unashamedly romantic and lyrical in its evocation of another vanished, pioneer epoch in the nation's history, the novel often verges on sentimentalism, but ultimately shows Cather's uncanny ability to make readers care deeply about the characters she creates. The novel was universally praised, sold better than any of Cather's other novels, and marked the high-water mark of her career.

PUBLIC HONORS AND PRIVATE TRIALS

In 1930, Cather was awarded the prestigious Howells Medal by the American Academy of the Arts for *Death Comes for the Archbishop*. Throughout this decade, she was awarded honorary degrees from Columbia, the University of California at Berkeley, Princeton, and her alma mater, the University of Nebraska. In the public sphere, there seemed no limit to what she could achieve. Yet beginning in 1928, an ongoing sequence of distressing events disrupted her private life. First, she found out that her home in Greenwich Village, where she had lived for fifteen years, was scheduled for demolition and that she would have to move. Cather would end up living in a hotel for the next five years. On March 3, 1928, Cather's father died of a heart attack, only a week after she had visited him in Nebraska. Charles Cather and his daughter had always been extremely close; in fact, her father and her brother Douglass were the two most important men in Willa Cather's life. To make matters worse, in December of the same year her mother suffered a serious stroke that left her paralyzed on one side and unable to speak. Her father's death had been terribly sudden, but the final illness of Cather's mother would be painfully drawn out; she finally died in 1931. Cather and her mother had had many personality clashes in her youth, but they had reconciled. With her mother's death and burial, Cather would never again visit Nebraska, the state that had formed her more than any other, and which she had fictionally made her own.

Cather managed to complete a novel, *Shadows on the Rock*, in 1931. Set in sixteenth-century Quebec, it marked a further leap into the more reassuring and stable world of the past, but lacked the incisive power of her previous fiction. The following year's publication of *Obscure Destinies* marked a stunning return to form. These three stories, which returned to a Nebraska setting, continued Cather's interest in and deep sympathy for those unnoticed and often forgotten individuals who, upon closer and more sympathetic examination, lead lives of almost saintly significance. The best-known story of the three, "Neighbor Rosicky," is loosely based on Annie Pavelka's husband, but it also incorporates aspects of Cather's father that she loved and admired. The tale sketches with deceptive yet utterly moving simplicity the twilight days of a father and husband who has chosen to nurture the love and comfort of his large family rather than pursue material prosperity and success like so many of his neighbors. Like Ántonia and Archbishop Latour, Rosicky has mastered the secret of contentment, and he, too, has been "dissolved into something complete and great." *Shadows on the Rock* was a relatively disappointing work, while *Obscure Destinies* was one of her finest; nevertheless, both were bestsellers, and Cather's popularity continued to grow.

Due to the wealth that sales of her novels had generated throughout the 1920s, Cather was not overly affected by the Great Depression of the 1930s, and in 1932 she rented a spacious apartment on upscale Park Avenue. Yet she had witnessed the depression's catastrophic consequences when she returned to Nebraska in 1931 to bury her mother, and she could not avoid the sight of so many homeless and unemployed people on the streets of New York. True to her commitment to the supposed "higher truths" of art at the expense

of politics, Cather remained remarkably detached from the
volatile political debates taking place in America at this time.
Just as she had never shown any real interest in journalists'
exposés of corporate corruption during her time at *McClure's*,
she remained politically conservative, and hostile to Franklin
D. Roosevelt's New Deal. This disengagement from the problems confronting Americans at this time drew severe criticism from left-wing critics who felt that times such as the
1930s compelled writers to confront society's injustices and
inequalities. Though she was by this time America's foremost
woman novelist, Cather was increasingly seen as something
of an anachronism—a skilled novelist who had always
evaded the difficulties of the present by turning to the conso-
lations of the past. As if to confirm these criticisms, Cather
herself became increasingly withdrawn and began to obses-
sively guard her privacy, restricting herself to a very small
circle of friends and retreating into her love of music.

Lucy Gayheart (1935), her next novel, was not, however, a
work that affirmed a figure from the past or celebrated a vanished way of life. A somber narrative of the thwarted life of
an artistic, beautiful, and romantic young woman, *Lucy Gayheart* seems to exist in opposition to Cather's third novel, *The
Song of the Lark*, whose plot concerns the growth and ultimate triumph of the artist. Critics were quick to note that
Cather's mastery of style and structure was as acute as ever,
but also charged that the novel lacked the emotional power
of her best work. Cather had returned to her early formula of
placing a young female at the center of a novel, but readers
have never been able to emotionally attach themselves to
Lucy as they have to Alexandra Bergson, Thea Kronberg, or
Ántonia Shimerda. Sales of *Lucy Gayheart* were modest,
mostly because novels were considered luxury items during
the depression and most Americans could not afford to buy
them. However, *Lucy Gayheart* earned Cather over $17,000—a
considerable sum of money at a time when millions were out
of work and a restaurant meal cost about fifty cents.

CATHER'S LAST DECADE

In the late 1930s Willa Cather divided her time between New
York City and a cottage she had had built on Grand Manan Island. In 1938 her life was once again shattered by the deaths of
her brother Douglass and Isabelle Hambourg, and she wondered in her letters to friends where and how she would find the
strength to go on. She did find some comfort in working on what

would be her final novel, *Sapphira and the Slave Girl.* True to Cather's fictional allegiance to the past, this novel went back beyond Nebraska to her own roots in rural Virginia. Visits to Back Creek Valley to research the novel and reacquaint herself with the novel's setting intensified her sense that her life was in its autumnal stage. Set in the Shenandoah Valley in 1856, the novel is based on an incident from her mother's family history, when her Grandmother Boak (Rachel Blake in the novel) had assisted in the escape of a slave girl to Canada. In a rather remarkable departure, the main female character, Sapphira, is a malicious, inexplicably cruel figure, and the novel is almost gothic in its fixation with motiveless evil. *Sapphira and the Slave Girl* was arguably Cather's best novel since *Death Comes for the Archbishop*, and it was an impressive way of ending a remarkable career as a novelist that had spanned nearly thirty years. Once again the novel was a best-seller, and reviews were uniformly enthusiastic.

Due to a serious injury to her right hand, which rendered her physically unable to write for sustained periods of time, Cather managed to complete only two short stories over the next seven years. For six years, she worked on and off on a novel set in medieval Avignon, France; however, it was unfinished when she died and her will ordered that the manuscript be destroyed. Although she had increasingly been accused of indifference to the world's problems, her letters from the early 1940s convey a sense of despair over the future of humanity, and she was certainly not blind to the threat Hitler and Stalin posed to Western civilization. New York during the war years had little appeal for her, and she was unable to go to Grand Manan Island due to wartime restrictions on travel. Yet one memorable occasion occurred in 1944, when Cather was awarded the National Institute for Arts and Letters gold medal for fiction. It was an award given only once a decade to acknowledge a writer's cumulative achievement; previous recipients included William Dean Howells and Edith Wharton. Another source of pleasure for Cather was her ongoing friendship with violin virtuoso Yehudi Menuhin and his family. Yet her brother Roscoe's death in 1945 seemed to usher in her own final surrender, even though her mental and physical vigor at seventy-two years of age was remarkable. Friends remembered that in Cather's last years, her conversation remained as lively and as incisive as ever, and her death from a massive cerebral hemorrhage on April 24, 1947, was completely unexpected.

Cather was buried in Jaffrey, New Hampshire, a place she had loved and where she had happily written some of her finest work. With her death came a brief eclipse in the attention paid to her fiction, though David Daiches wrote an excellent critical introduction in 1951, and two years later E.K. Brown completed what is still a highly regarded biography. Poet Wallace Stevens once commented that in her fiction Cather "takes so much pains to conceal her sophistication that it is easy to miss her quality." Since the 1980s, critics and readers have increasingly come to appreciate the multi-layered complexity and the stylistic ingenuity of Cather's work. Her reputation continues to rise, and she is now viewed, along with Faulkner, Hemingway, Fitzgerald, and Steinbeck, as one of American literature's undisputed giants.

WORKS CITED

L. Brent Bohlke, ed., *Willa Cather in Person: Interviews, Speeches, Letters.* Lincoln: University of Nebraska Press, 1986.

William M. Curtin, ed., *The World and the Parish: Willa Cather's Articles and Reviews, 1893–1902.* Lincoln: University of Nebraska Press, 1970.

Sharon O'Brien, *Willa Cather: The Emerging Voice.* Oxford: Oxford University Press, 1987.

Holly Stevens, ed., *Letters of Wallace Stevens.* New York: Knopf, 1966.

CHARACTERS AND PLOT

Jim Burden. The novel's narrator and arguably its central character. After growing up in Nebraska, Jim has become a successful New York lawyer. Jim is sensitive, intelligent, and has a romantic nature, which makes him feel more strongly than anyone else the beauty and vitality of Ántonia Shimerda. Although Jim is overwhelmingly sympathetic toward Ántonia, readers should be aware that his understanding of her is somewhat limited by his upbringing and his own prejudices. He often expresses disappointment in Ántonia, because she has turned out differently than he expected her to. Often Ántonia is less a person to him than an idealized representative of his youth and what for him was best about frontier life. Only at the end of the novel does Jim realize that Ántonia has always understood what she wanted from life and has been uncompromising in following her own destiny. Unlike Jim, who has a childless and unsatisfactory marriage, Ántonia is surrounded by an abundance of both children and love.

The Burden Grandparents. Jim's grandparents take him in when he is orphaned at ten years of age. Although they play a minor role in the novel, they are portrayed as kind, decent, and deeply religious people. Jim sees his grandmother as an extremely strong woman, while he is in awe of his distinguished-looking grandfather. More established and prosperous than the recent immigrant settlers, Jim's grandparents willingly help the Shimerdas through the difficult first year after their arrival, and they have a special affection for Ántonia.

Gaston Cleric. Jim Burden's passionate and inspiring professor at the university in Lincoln. He befriends and eventually invites Jim to join him at Harvard; however, his health is poor, and he later dies of pneumonia.

The Cutters. Wick Cutter is a rapacious moneylender, well known for exploiting poor immigrant farmers. He also has a reputation as a gambler and dissolute womanizer, and his long-suffering wife detests him but will not leave. When Ántonia goes to work for the Cutters, he tries unsuccessfully to rape her. Years later, Jim is told that Cutter shot himself after murdering his wife as she slept in their bed.

Larry Donovan. Ántonia's would-be husband, who abandons her in Denver without marrying her. A railroad conductor, he is dishonest and manipulative, and it appears that everyone can see that except Ántonia.

Otto Fuchs and Jake. Men employed as farmhands by Jim's grandparents, they are unswervingly loyal to Jim's grandparents and kind to Jim. Jim is especially taken with Otto, who has lived a wild life in the West previous to his employment with the Burdens. After Jim's grandparents move to Black Hawk, Otto and Jake decide to go prospecting out West, and Jim never sees them again.

Anton Cuzak. Ántonia's husband and a cousin of Anton Jelinek. After making a living as a shoemaker in Vienna, Cuzak emigrates to America, living first in Florida and then in Nebraska, where he meets and marries Ántonia. Like Ántonia's father, he is a cultured man more at home in the cities of Europe than the farms of Nebraska. However, unlike Mr. Shimerda, he manages to adapt to the farming life, and he and Ántonia have a happy and successful marriage.

The Harlings. A prosperous Black Hawk family that befriends Jim and employs Ántonia in their house until she leaves to work for the Cutters. A grain merchant, Mr. Harling is the wealthiest man in Black Hawk, but Jim finds him cold and arrogant, and is glad that he is often away on business. On the other hand, Mrs. Harling is much admired by Jim. She has a forceful character and is a cultured perfectionist. Like Jim, she, too, is much taken with Ántonia, but is bitterly disappointed when Ántonia resigns her position with the family. Frances Harling is the eldest daughter, and is seen as both an extremely shrewd businesswoman and a humane, concerned advocate for immigrant farmers. The other Harling children—Charley, Julia and Sally—appear infrequently and are not developed as complete characters.

Anton Jelinek. A likeable Bohemian immigrant who arrives to help the Shimerdas after Mr. Shimerda kills himself. He later settles in Black Hawk and establishes a saloon.

Lena Lingard. A child of a Norwegian immigrant farming

family, Lena leaves the farm for Black Hawk as soon as she can to become a dressmaker. An attractive and well-groomed woman, Lena draws men's affections. Yet she is fiercely independent and maintains she will never marry because she has seen how marriage and a family have worn out her mother, for whom she cares deeply. Later Lena moves to Lincoln while Jim is studying at the university. Jim, like others before him, is strongly attracted to Lena, but their relationship ends when Jim leaves to study at Harvard. Lena eventually moves to San Francisco, where she becomes a successful dressmaker.

Ántonia Shimerda. Though Ántonia is often absent for significant periods of time throughout the novel, she remains the novel's focus. Throughout the novel, Cather creates a close correlation between Ántonia and the subtle beauties of the prairie, and Ántonia increasingly becomes a kind of earth-mother figure, possessing as she does the quality of an endlessly life-giving force. Her life is full of adversity—her father commits suicide when she is fourteen, her fiancé Larry Donovan abandons her while she is pregnant, and the threat of poverty is always near. However, Ántonia manages against all odds to find lasting contentment, something that eludes so many of Willa Cather's characters. With her large family and a farm that has prospered after a long and exhausting struggle, she renews Jim's sense of hope and purpose in his own life. Jim is correct when he observes that Ántonia "had that something which fires the imagination, could stop one's breath for a moment by a look or gesture that somehow revealed the meaning in common things."

The Shimerdas. Upon their arrival in Nebraska, the Shimerda family is composed of Mr. and Mrs. Shimerda and their four children, including Ántonia. A musician and tailor, Mr. Shimerda is a cultured and sensitive man who was respected and liked in his home country; however, he is completely out of place in Nebraska and cannot adapt to the harsh realities of frontier life. Homesick and in despair, he commits suicide in the middle of the family's terrible first winter in Nebraska. Mrs. Shimerda is presented in very unsympathetic terms. Calculating, demanding, and at times hysterical, whenever she appears Jim has no hesitation in expressing his contempt for her; unlike her husband, though, she is a survivor. The eldest son, Ambrosch, is a strong and competent farmer, but he is also sullen and cruel. He works Ántonia to exhaustion in the fields, and wants to kill Ántonia's illegitimate child when it is born. The other two Shimerda children, Yulka and Marek (who is mentally handicapped and eventually institutionalized), barely appear in the novel and are mentioned only briefly.

Tiny Soderball. Another of the "hired girls" who moves to Black Hawk to find work and support her family. When Tiny eventually leaves Black Hawk, she has an adventurous life operating a boardinghouse in Alaska during the 1890s gold rush. She makes a fortune and settles in San Francisco, but Jim observes that in her middle age she appears to be interested only in making money.

The Widow Steavens. A kindly woman who takes over the Burdens' farm when they move to Black Hawk. Like the Burdens, she becomes very fond of Ántonia, and it is she who tells Jim the sad tale of Ántonia's seduction and abandonment by Larry Donovan.

THE PLOT

My Ántonia begins with an unnamed character recalling a train ride he (or she) took with Jim Burden across the Midwest the previous summer. We find out from this character that Jim Burden is a successful New York lawyer. Something of a romantic, Jim's spirit has been compromised by a loveless marriage to a wealthy New York socialite. However, his job often takes him back to the Midwest, where he grew up and which he deeply loves. As the train makes its way across the prairie, the narrator and Jim recall the uniqueness of their respective upbringings in Black Hawk, Nebraska, and their conversation repeatedly returns to a girl who "seemed to mean to us the country, the conditions, the whole adventure of our childhood." This girl is Ántonia Shimerda. Jim relates that he has renewed his friendship with Ántonia after a gap of twenty years, and that often as he has traveled across the country by train he has written down his recollections of her when she was young. Jim's anonymous acquaintance expresses enthusiastic interest in reading this account of Ántonia, and, months later in New York, Jim shows up with a completed manuscript. Jim modestly cautions that his memoir is not very well organized—that he "simply wrote down pretty much all that her name recalls to me." The manuscript has no title, but after some deliberation Jim writes "My Ántonia" on the cover, and his narrative of Ántonia Shimerda begins.

The first book of *My Ántonia* is called "The Shimerdas," and finds Jim at age ten. Recently orphaned in Virginia, Jim is on a train bound for Black Hawk, Nebraska, to begin a new life with his grandparents. The conductor tells Jim there is an immigrant family on board that is also heading for Black Hawk, and that they have a girl about Jim's age whom he should go and see. Jim is shy and refuses, but this is the first mention of Ántonia Shimerda, who will have such a significant impact on Jim's life. After what seems to Jim an endless journey, the train finally arrives in Black Hawk, and he is struck by the vast emptiness of the land. To Jim, "There seemed to be nothing to see; no fences, no creeks or trees, no hills or fields. . . . There was nothing but land: not a country at all, but the material out of which countries are made." Jim feels isolated and terribly alone, thinking that in such a place, not even his dead parents will be here to look down on him.

The next morning, Jim sees his grandparents' farm for the first time, and he quickly comes to terms with his new environment. The Burdens soon come to know the Shimerdas, the family that arrived the same night as Jim. The Shimerdas are the first Bohemian family to settle in the region, and Mr. and Mrs. Shimerda have two sons and two daughters. Trusting and not at all knowledgeable about the land they intend to farm, the family has already been exploited by a fellow Bohemian, Peter Krajiek, who has sold them his farm, its animals, and implements for a lot more than they are worth. Jim and Ántonia quickly become friends, and Mr. Shimerda encourages Jim to teach Ántonia English. The two spend a lot of time exploring the prairie; in one dramatic scene Jim kills an enormous rattlesnake, which earns him the everlasting respect of Ántonia. These days are idyllic for Jim and Ántonia as they discover the subtle beauties of the land; however, the Shimerdas are struggling with their farm, and a harsh winter is on the way.

A cultured and sensitive man, Mr. Shimerda finds it particularly difficult to adapt to farming life in a new country. The only friends he has in the area are two Russians—Peter and Pavel—who are barely surviving on their own farm. One day Jim and Ántonia accompany Mr. Shimerda to see Pavel, who has fallen gravely ill. On his sickbed, Pavel tells a terrible tale from many years ago, when he and Peter lived in Russia. When the two were young men, they accompanied a bride and groom from their wedding feast to their lodgings in the next town. On the way to the town, the wedding party's sleighs were set on by an enormous pack of hungry wolves. The situation grew increasingly desperate, with one sleigh after another falling to the pack. Finally, Pavel determines that the only way for his sleigh to outrun the wolves is to throw the bride and groom off, thereby lightening the load. After a struggle he succeeds, and he and Peter make it to the town alive. However, because of their terrible deed they are run out of their town and branded outcasts wherever they go. After years of wandering all over Russia, they finally saved enough money to move to America. Soon after he confesses this tale to Mr. Shimerda, Pavel dies, the farm is auctioned off, and Peter disappears.

On the heels of this terrible tale, winter arrives. As the weather grows increasingly bitter, the fortunes of the Shimerdas drastically decline. Because they arrived too late to plant a crop for that year, they have barely any food and have nearly run out of money. Hearing of their difficulties, the Burdens visit them one day with supplies, and are appalled at the squalor in which the Shimerdas are living. At this point, the difference between the Burdens and the Shimerdas becomes very clear. Whereas the Burdens live comfortably in the only wood house in their district, the Shimerdas are living in a hole dug in the ground and are nearly starving. As the winter progresses, Mr. Shimerda becomes more and more withdrawn and depressed. In his home country he had been a successful and respected man, but he has neither the knowledge nor ability to survive in Nebraska, and with the departure of Peter he has no friends. One morning in January, Jim awakes and is told that Mr. Shimerda has killed himself. Krajiek is briefly suspected of foul play, but there is finally no doubt that Ántonia's father was driven to commit suicide by homesickness and despair.

After the funeral of Mr. Shimerda, the novel moves on to the following spring, and the Shimerdas prepare to plant their corn. Ántonia no longer has time to see Jim, as she is too busy helping her brother Ambrosch break in the land. Jim hopes she will be able to go to school with him, but she is already tied to the soil, telling Jim that "School is alright for little boys. I help make this land one good farm." Jim is hurt by her new attitude; already their lives are drifting apart because of their different circumstances. Some weeks later Jim and Jake, one of his grandfather's farmhands, visit the Shimerdas to retrieve a horse collar they have lent them. Ambrosch Shimerda, a sullen and greedy character, flippantly returns the horse collar in terrible condition. He and Jake argue over it, and finally they fight. Jim vows never to speak to Ántonia again, but by the middle of the summer, Ántonia has come to help Jim's grandmother around the Burden farm, and their friendship is renewed. Yet Ántonia knows that Jim and her family will take divergent paths, and the section ends with her saying to Jim that "Things will be easy for you. But they will be hard for us."

The novel's second section, "The Hired Girls," jumps ahead a little over two years and shifts the novel's location from the Burden and Shimerda farms to the town of Black Hawk. Jim's grandparents decide to retire from farming and settle in town, and they want Jim to receive a better education than he had at the country school. Jim does not see Ántonia at all for nine months, until she takes a job with the Harling family. In this section, the Harlings become the focus of Jim's life, since they have three children his age and the house is often an inviting place for family and social gatherings. The rarely seen Mr. Harling is a grain merchant, and the most successful businessman in the area, while his cultured, energetic wife runs the house and raises their four children. From this point on Jim sees Ántonia, now seventeen, nearly every day. We are soon introduced to Lena Lingard and Tiny Soderball, two immigrant farm girls who are determined to make lives for themselves in town. Ántonia, Lena, and Tiny constitute the core of the "hired girls," who become the source of so much attention and notoriety when a dancing pavilion comes to Black Hawk the next summer.

Jim Burden is quite aware of the crushing conformity and need to be seen as behaving respectably that characterizes most of the residents of Black Hawk. With the establishment of the dancing pavilion in town, the immigrant girls—beautiful and bursting with vitality—suddenly attract a great deal of attention from young, middle-class men who customarily look down on immigrant farming families. The dancing pavilion becomes a meeting ground and source of tension among all classes. Ultimately the need for "respectability" wins out, and the middle-class men end up courting girls who have money but, in Jim's opinion, none of the personality of an Ántonia or a Lena. Finally Ántonia's obsession with the dances gets her in trouble with Mr. Harling, and when she is forced to make a choice between forgoing the dances or keeping her position with the Harlings, she leaves. Ántonia explains to Mrs. Harling that she will only be young once, and that "A girl like me has got to take her good times while she can." She ends up taking a position with Wick Cutter, an evil and lecherous Black Hawk moneylender.

While Ántonia lives for dancing and dressing as elegantly as she can, Jim begins to chafe under the boredom and restrictions of small-town life. In a particularly angry yet powerful passage, he proclaims that "This guarded mode of existence was like living under a tyranny. People's speech, their voices, their very glances, became furtive and repressed. Every individual taste, every natural appetite, was bridled by caution." Word gets back to Jim's grandmother that he is going to disreputable dances and will therefore turn out bad, but all he wants to do is be with the "hired girls," whom he finds more interesting than the bland and vacuous girls from his own social set. Out of his love for his grandmother he promises not to go again, which further restricts the social options available to him. Jim becomes determined to escape Black Hawk and begins studying harder than ever so that he can go to the university. Meanwhile, Ántonia has begun to regularly see a railroad conductor named Larry Donovan.

After Jim graduates, he spends one memorable day at a country picnic with the "hired girls," where they talk about their dreams and their futures. At the end of the day, the sun sets behind a plough standing in a field, magnifying it for a short, glorious instant, and it seems to represent the heroism of the entire pioneering enterprise, of which the "hired girls" are such outstanding representatives. Instead of ending the section on this highly symbolic and uplifting note, though, Cather returns to Black Hawk, where a disturbing incident takes place. Ántonia tells Jim's grandmother that the Cutters are going away for a few days, and she is frightened of being alone in the house, especially in light of Mr. Cutter's strange behavior toward her. Jim agrees to stay in the Cutter house in Ántonia's place, and on the third night he is awakened by Mr. Cutter's return. He has returned to rape Ántonia and has instead found Jim. After a brief, violent scuffle, Jim escapes, and "The Hired Girls" section ends.

The novel's third section, "Lena Lingard," moves to Lincoln, Nebraska, where Jim is continuing his studies. Although he is stimulated and inspired by the teaching of his professor Gaston Cleric, Jim misses the people and places of his youth and begins to realize how profoundly they have shaped the person he has become. While engaged in his studies of the poet Virgil, he comes to realize that young women such as Ántonia and Lena embody all the classical virtues of country life that this poet of ancient Rome wrote about so many centuries earlier. During his second year in

Lincoln, he is surprised and delighted to be visited by Lena Lingard, who has moved to the city to begin her own dress-making business. The two begin to spend a lot of time together, and have something of a platonic courtship. Lena, however, makes it clear to Jim that she will never marry, because she cherishes her independence and never wants to have to be accountable to anybody. Having grown up with many brothers and sisters in a poor farming household, and having seen how it completely wore her own mother out, Lena wants to concentrate on her already successful business. Jim's time in Lincoln with Lena comes to an end when Cleric is offered a position at Harvard, and he in turn offers Jim a place there as a student. Jim's grandfather agrees that Jim can go to Harvard, too, if he wishes; Cleric urges him to do so, maintaining that if he continues to see Lena he will eventually abandon his studies altogether. Somewhat meekly, Jim agrees, and this section of the novel comes to an end.

During this section, Ántonia has not appeared at all, but Jim has heard that she has continued to see Larry Donovan, for whom Jim has a strong dislike. Lena agrees, but she quite rightly observes "if (Ántonia) once likes people, she won't hear anything against them." In the novel's fourth section, "The Pioneer Woman's Story," two more years have passed and Jim is about to enter Harvard Law School. The summer before he will begin his legal studies, he returns to Black Hawk, already knowing that Ántonia has moved to Denver, Colorado, to marry Larry Donovan, that he has deserted her, and that she has returned to her mother's farm pregnant. Jim admits that he is "bitterly disappointed" in Ántonia, and says that he could forgive her "if she hadn't thrown herself away on such a cheap sort of fellow."

Jim finally hears the full story from the Widow Steavens, a woman who took over the Burden farm once they moved to town. He learns from Mrs. Steavens that Donovan never married Ántonia, and that he is now probably in Mexico. Yet Jim finds that, although Ántonia rarely goes into Black Hawk and is trapped on her mother and Ambrosch's farm, she is proud of her child and is "a natural-born mother." Jim becomes determined to see Ántonia again, and the next day rides out to the Shimerda farm. Jim notes that Ántonia is thin and looks tired, but that "there was a new kind of gravity in her face." Jim's sense of disappointment in Ántonia soon evaporates, and he tells her that he always thinks of her and that she is terribly important to him: "You influence my likes and dislikes, all my tastes, hundreds of times when I don't realize it. You really are a part of me." This section ends with a longing on Jim's part for the innocent days of his and Ántonia's youth, and Cather returns to a vivid description of the landscape, with the sun setting dramatically in the west as the two part ways.

The novel's final section, "Cuzak's Boys," moves forward twenty years. Jim has not seen Ántonia at all in that time. He has heard from Lena and Tiny Soderball (who after an adventurous life in Alaska has settled in San Francisco and is a very wealthy woman) that Ántonia has married, has had many children, and has had to struggle a great deal to make a new farm. Jim admits that he has avoided seeing Ántonia, maintaining that "I did not want to find her aged and broken; I really dreaded it. In the course of twenty crowded years one parts with many illusions. I did not wish to lose the early ones." Finally Lena, who like Tiny has settled in San Francisco and become very successful in business, urges him to visit Ántonia. Jim agrees to do so, and once he arrives, his fears that Ántonia has been beaten down and broken by life's hardships are quickly put to rest. Certainly Ántonia has aged, but for Jim "She was there, in the full vigour of her personality, battered but not diminished. . . . Ántonia had not lost the fire of life." She has a large and loving family, and with her husband she has obviously struggled hard to build a beautiful farm that supplies her family's needs in abundance. Ántonia proudly introduces Jim to all her children and shows him the family's fruit cellar and orchard. The next day Jim meets Anton Cuzak, Ántonia's husband, when he returns with their oldest son from a fair in a distant town. Jim sees immediately that there is an easy harmony between Cuzak and Ántonia, and once again he perceives that Ántonia somehow has the gift of making the most of the simplest things in life. When Jim finally leaves, he feels enlivened and reinvigorated by Ántonia's family and his renewed friendship. He drives into Black Hawk and feels it has changed for the worse, since many of his former acquaintances have either died or moved on. His thoughts keep returning to Ántonia, who meant so much to him, and the novel ends with his affirmation that "Whatever we had missed, we possessed together the precious, the incommunicable past."

CHAPTER 1

The Autobiographical and Historical Background of *My Ántonia*

READINGS ON
MY ÁNTONIA

Annie Pavelka: Willa Cather's Inspiration for Ántonia

James L. Woodress

This excerpt from the definitive biography of Willa Cather begins with the author's visit in 1916 to Annie Pavelka, a childhood friend of Cather's who had by this time married, established a farm, and raised a large family. According to biographer James L. Woodress, it was this reunion that served as the starting point for the creation of Ántonia Shimerda. Woodress also illustrates how, in creating Ántonia, Cather was able to draw on a full store of her own memories and experiences growing up on the Great Plains, thereby creating a novel that is almost autobiographical in its apparent artlessness. James L. Woodress is an emeritus professor of English at the University of California at Davis.

Nebraska that summer (1916) was blisteringly hot. The amorous lovers of Dante were no more scourged by fire than were the dwellers of the corn country, she wrote [her friend Elizabeth] Sergeant; but corn took a terrific amount of heat, she added, and they all panted resignedly under the magnificent fire as the crops matured. Sometime in September or October Cather must have driven out into the Bohemian country, as she usually did, to visit her old friend Annie Pavelka. This may have been the trip that Jim Burden takes in the final book of *My Ántonia* when he sees Ántonia, now middle-aged, married, and surrounded by her large brood of children. The idea of her novel had not yet come to her, however, and she spent the fall working on "The Blue Mesa." Two months after getting to Red Cloud she was still making notes for it, but the materials seemed intractable. The experience was too recent for use and needed to remain a few years in the deep well of her unconscious. . . .

She arrived in New York, however, with the idea for *My Ántonia*. She wrote R.L. Scaife at Houghton Mifflin the following March that as soon as she had returned from the West, she had put aside "The Blue Mesa" to take up work on a new novel, a western story about the same length as *O Pioneers!* and with a somewhat similar background. In three months she had gotten half way through the first draft, and she thought she might be ready to send the manuscript to Boston by mid-June. She wanted to know the latest date possible to make fall publication, and by April she was already writing about the illustrations for the new novel. But she was too optimistic by far, and it was another fourteen months before she completed the book. . . .

In one sense Cather had been preparing to write *My Ántonia* for a third of a century. She had known the model for its fictional heroine, Annie Sadilek, later Pavelka, ever since she was a child in Red Cloud, and . . . the story of Annie's father's suicide was one of the first stories she had heard in Nebraska. As she looked back in her old age, she felt that the character of Ántonia was the embodiment of all her feelings about the early immigrants in the prairie country, and it seemed then that she must have been destined to write this novel if she ever wrote anything. When Margaret Lawrence's *School of Femininity* appeared in 1936 with a perceptive chapter on Cather, she agreed with its thesis: she could only write successfully when she wrote about people or places she loved. The characters she created could be cranky or queer or foolhardy or rash, but they had to have something to them that thrilled her and warmed her heart.

Annie Sadilek Pavelka was such a person. Cather told an interviewer in 1921 that one of the people who had interested her most when she was a child was the Bohemian hired girl who worked for one of their neighbors. "She was one of the truest artists I ever knew in the keenness and sensitiveness of her enjoyment, in her love of people and in her willingness to take pains." After Cather left journalism and began writing novels, she visited the Bohemian country during her summer visits to Red Cloud and saw Annie and her family on their farm. The lives of the Pavelkas and their neighbors seemed to her like stories out of a book that went on and on year after year like *War and Peace*. Whenever she went back to Nebraska, her friends filled her in on the details of the narrative that had taken place in her absence.

THE CHOICE OF A MALE NARRATOR

Once she decided to make Annie the central figure in her novel, she had to work out the narrative technique to present her. She chose a first-person point of view because she believed that novels of feeling, such as *My Ántonia*, were best narrated by a character in the story. Novels of action, on the other hand, should be told in the third person, using the omniscient author as narrator. But who should the first-person teller of the tale be? She told an interviewer that she rejected Annie's lover as narrator because "my Ántonia deserved something better than the *Saturday Evening Post* sort of stuff." But she wanted a male narrator because, as she explained, most of what she knew about Annie came from talks with young men: "She had a fascination for them, and they used to be with her whenever they could. They had to manage it on the sly because she was only a hired girl." Thus Cather created as narrator Jim Burden, whose age, experience, and personal history closely parallel her own. He tells the story as an adult reminiscence. Of course, Cather had been using male narrators in her short fiction for a long time, and there was no novelty for her in this invention.

She felt obliged, however, to defend her use of a male narrator. When her old friend and editor Will Owen Jones asked her why she had done it, she repeated her explanation that she had gotten her material from young men, then added further rationalization by reminding Jones of her experience in writing McClure's autobiography. [S.S. McClure was the publisher of *McClure's* magazine, where Cather worked as an editor from 1905–1913.] She had been so successful in masquerading as McClure then that she felt confident in doing an entire novel from a male perspective. When she first began writing the autobiography, she found it awfully hampering to be McClure all the time, but in the end it became fascinating to work within the limits and color of the personality she knew so well. Even Mrs. McClure and John Phillips, McClure's college classmate and former business partner, found the presentation completely convincing.

Once she had decided on her narrative voice and the first-person method, she further planned to avoid any formal structuring of the novel. Jim Burden's memories, which, of course, were her memories, would shape the narrative. She would avoid the opportunities for melodrama that the materials certainly contained and dwell lightly on the incidents that most novelists would ordinarily emphasize. The story would be made up of little, everyday happenings for the most part, for such events made up the bulk of most people's lives. It would be the other side of the rug, the pattern that is supposed not to count. There would be no love affair, no courtship, no marriage, no broken heart, no struggle for success. "I knew I'd ruin my material if I put it in the usual fictional pattern. I just used it the way I thought absolutely true." The result was the creation of a novel that gives the impression of real autobiography rather than fiction. Since the invented narrator is not a professional writer, the apparent artlessness of his memories seems perfectly logical, and the reader is willing to suspend his belief that he is in the presence of a perfectly controlled art. . . .

A Drama of Memory

More than most writers, Cather presents readers with the chance to compare biographical data with its transmutation into art. There is a great deal more factual basis in *My Ántonia* than the bare story outline of the title character and the narrator. The town of Black Hawk is again Red Cloud, and the Nebraska farmlands again provide the locale. Ántonia's farm house still stands in the country north of Red Cloud with the fruit cave a few yards from the back door. Jim's grandparents, as we have seen, are drawn from life, the entire Miner family play roles in the story, and Herbert Bates appears as Gaston Cleric, Jim's college teacher. In addition to the main characters and incidents, minor figures and events also are rooted in actuality. The black pianist, Blind d'Arnault, who plays in Black Hawk, was drawn from a real Blind Tom, whom Cather heard in Lincoln, and a Blind Boone, whom she probably heard in Red Cloud. The visitor to the town today can see the home of Wick Cutter, who in actuality was a loan-shark named Bentley and apparently as evil and unsavory as Cather makes him. The hotel-keeping Mrs. Gardener in the novel was a real Mrs. Holland, and the man who fathered Ántonia's first child out of wedlock was James William Murphy.

After the novel appeared, Cather was pestered by literal-minded readers wanting to know where she got this and

A MOMENT OF ARTISTIC CLARITY

Elizabeth Shepley Sergeant, a close friend and early biographer of Willa Cather, recounts a memorable day when Cather visited her New York apartment and dramatically revealed how she wished to approach her newest creation, Ántonia Shimerda.

In the spring of 1916, I had the first inkling that Willa had a new story in mind. I never asked questions—she was the initiator of any communication about an unborn or unfinished work.

She had not been able to forget that, in these war days, the youth of Europe, its finest flower, was dying. Perhaps our American youth had also been designed for sacrifice—by now we feared so. But a growing vital work, with Willa, usually took precedence, even in her thoughts, over the life around her.

She had come in for tea at a small apartment facing south on a garden, in the East Sixties where I was living. As it was not far from Central Park, she arrived flushed and alert from one of her swift wintry walks. I think of her as always wearing red-brown fur in winter in those years; it made her hair shine, and she had the warmth, charm, assurance, and fullness of being that allied her, despite her individual direction, with *the* American woman in her forties. She said more than once to me that nobody under forty could ever really believe in either death or degeneration. She herself carried that physical nonchalance right on through her fifties. . . .

She then suddenly leaned over—and this is something I remembered clearly when *My Ántonia* came into my hands, at last, in 1918—and set an old Sicilian apothecary jar of mine, filled with orange-brown flowers of scented stock, in the middle of a bare, round, antique table.

"I want my new heroine to be like this—like a rare object in the middle of a table, which one may examine from all sides."

She moved the lamp so that light streamed brightly down on my Taormina jar, with its glazed orange and blue design.

"I want her to stand out—like this—like this—because she *is* the story."

Saying this her fervent, enthusiastic voice faltered and her eyes filled with tears.

Someone you knew in your childhood, I ventured.

She nodded, but did not say more.

Elizabeth Shepley Sergeant, *Willa Cather: A Memoir.* New York: J.P. Lippincott, 1953, pp. 138–40.

where she got that. The people in Red Cloud were continually playing guessing games with her characters and incidents. It exasperated her, but she should have expected her drama of memory to provoke this kind of a response. Sometimes she was patient and discussed her sources with friends—sometimes she even answered letters from students—but usually her reaction was annoyance. Often she did not know where she got things, and after *My Ántonia* was published, her father pointed out half a dozen different incidents that were based on things she had done, seen, or heard of with him, all of which she thought she had invented.

One such episode was the story within a story of the two Russians, Pavel and Peter, and the wolves. It illustrates the way Cather's creative imagination worked, as she fashioned her fictional materials from her memories. The wolf story probably came both from herself and from hearing the tale in her father's presence. It is a gruesome account of a wedding party in Russia traveling from one village to another in the dead of winter. Six sledges are attacked by wolves, and one by one they are overturned and the occupants killed by the beasts. Finally the only sledge left is the one carrying Pavel, Peter, and the bride and groom. Just before the sledge reaches the safety of the village, Pavel throws the bride and groom to the wolves. For this inhuman act Pavel and Peter are ostracized and forced to leave Russia for America. This story is a folk tale that folklorists have collected from the oral tradition of Nebraska immigrants in the identical version that Cather uses. She no doubt heard the story from the farm people she knew. At the same time, her idea that she made up the story perhaps comes from having seen a well-known painting by Paul Powis depicting wolves attacking a sledge or from a poem by Browning, "Ivan Ivanovitch," which tells a similar tale. Since Cather took a year-long course in Browning at the University of Nebraska, it seems reasonable to conclude that she remembered the poem.

Cather always insisted that her characters were not drawn from real life but were only suggested by people she knew, or they were composites. You can never get it through people's heads, she wrote Carrie Sherwood, that a story is made out of an emotion or an excitement and is not made out of the legs and arms and faces of one's friends. There was one exception to this, however, in the character of Mrs.

Harling. Cather was working on "The Hired Girls" when she read of Mrs. Miner's death in a Red Cloud newspaper. She made a deliberate effort to remember her tricks of voice and gesture, and she made Mrs. Harling a clear little snapshot of Mrs. Miner as she first knew her. All of the mothers in her fiction, she admitted, had a little of Mrs. Miner in them, but this fictional portrait was unique, and she hoped the Miner daughters would like it. She dedicated the novel to Carrie and Irene "in memory of affections old and true." The older one grows, she added, the clearer one's early impressions somehow become.

My Ántonia's Enduring Success

Few novels are likely to be read longer than *My Ántonia*. In it character, theme, setting, myth, and incident are combined into a narrative of great emotional power. The prose is limpid, evocative, the product of Cather's nearly three decades of learning to master her instrument. For many readers it is her greatest work. She knew she had done well with this book and told Carrie Sherwood in 1938 that "the best thing I've done is *My Ántonia*. I feel I've made a contribution to American letters with that book." On other occasions she gave this precedence to *Death Comes for the Archbishop*. In 1943 [Cather's publisher] Greenslet wrote her that *My Ántonia* was a novel to cherish. It had sold twenty-five hundred copies in the previous year, and he didn't think there was another novel published a quarter of a century before that had continued to do so well. These were all copies in the regular hardcover edition, and this in the middle of the war. Through the years the novel has always sold steadily and never has been out of print.

Everything went right in this work—a great concept executed with consummate artistry—and it goes well beyond any of her first three novels. While Alexandra Bergson is the strong, intelligent tamer of the wild land, Thea Kronborg with the godlike name the climber of Olympus, Ántonia Shimerda is the mother of races. She is the most heroic figure of all, both the Madonna of the Wheat Fields and the symbol of the American westering myth. Although there are somber tones in her story, it ends on an affirmative note. The suicide of her father, the hard toil on the prairie farm, the desertion by her lover— these things have receded into the past by the final chapter, and what remains at the end is the indelible picture of Ántonia and her children: "It was no wonder that her sons stood tall and straight. She was a rich mine of life, like the founders of early races." Even after several readings one cannot finish this novel without being moved.

Cather managed to avoid the pitfalls inherent in her narrative method. Jim Burden as an unreliable narrator, childless, unhappily married to a promoter of avant garde causes, a man who jots down at random his memories of his youth, could have produced a story excessively sentimental; but he did not. There is the aura of nostalgia frequently found in Cather's fiction, but the sentiment does not become sentimentality. Cather escapes this by her usual juxtaposition of contrasts; in this case good and evil are alternated. Jim Burden's golden memories are constantly being interrupted by the sterner realities. The idyl of Jim's boyhood is punctuated by the rattlesnake episode, the suicide of Ántonia's father, the deviltries of Wick Cutter, the meanness of Ántonia's older brother, the horrible story of Pavel and Peter, and Ántonia's seduction. The cruel and ugly scenes and characters balance nicely the pleasant memories: the wonderful first autumn, the happy Christmas scene, Mrs. Harling's music, the picnic, the exhilarating talk of Gaston Cleric, the final visit to Ántonia's farm.

One of the remarkable aspects of this novel is its appeal to unsophisticated and sophisticated readers alike. The college freshman who has read very little is just as captivated by *My Ántonia* as his English professor who has read everything from Beowulf to author Thomas Kennerly Wolfe. The freshman finds a simple, human story dealing with genuine people facing recognizable problems. He can relate to it; he is touched by the real feeling evoked; he can read it without a dictionary or recourse to someone else's notes or annotations. The professor finds in the novel, besides a moving story, a richness of allusion, myth, and symbol presented by one of the great stylists of this century. This wide appeal results from Cather's blending together her native experience and her wide knowledge of European literature and culture. Her memories of Nebraska give her novel color, romance, emotional content; her general culture supplies texture, profundity, intellectual content. Together they make a literary classic. . . .

MY ÁNTONIA'S CRITICAL RECEPTION

The novel appeared in late September 1918, when the country was preoccupied with the final days of World War I, which ended with the Armistice on November 11. The book did not become a best seller, though it sold moderately well, passing the five thousand mark by Christmas and reaching about eight thousand by the time it had been out a year. Cather's royalties for the first twelve months amounted to less than two thousand dollars, however; not enough to support her while she wrote another novel. By the end of 1919 it was only selling five hundred copies a year and by late 1920 it was briefly unavailable due to a printers' strike. But the reviewers were nearly unanimous in their praise and recognized the novel as a significant contribution to American letters. Greenslet recorded in his memoirs that when he read the book in manuscript he experienced "the most thrilling shock of recognition of the real thing of any manuscript" he ever received.

H.L. Mencken again led the chorus with two reviews in consecutive issues of the *Smart Set*. *My Ántonia*, he wrote, was merely one more "step upward in the career of a writer who has labored with the utmost patience and industry, and won every foot of the way by hard work." He again praised her earlier novels, but *My Ántonia* was a sudden leap forward, "not only the best [novel] done by Miss Cather herself, but also one of the best that any American has ever done." Then he continued with the utmost enthusiasm: "It is intelligent; it is moving. The means that appear in it are means perfectly adapted to its end. Its people are unquestionably real. Its background is brilliantly vivid. It has form, grace, good literary manners. In a word, it is a capital piece of writing, and it will be heard of long after the baroque balderdash now touted on the 'book pages' is forgotten."

Randolph Bourne, whom Cather thought the best reviewer in the business, was equally pleased: "Miss Cather convinces because she knows her story and carries it along with the surest touch. It has all the artistic simplicity of material that has been patiently shaped until everything irrelevant has been scraped away." He concluded his review with the opinion that Cather "has taken herself out of the rank of provincial writers and given us something we can fairly class with the modern literary art the world over that is earnestly and richly interpreting the spirit of youth." The *New York Sun* carried a long, anonymous notice that particularly pleased Cather because the reviewer really understood what she was doing and made all the right comments.

"The most extraordinary thing about *My Ántonia* is the author's surrender of the usual methods of fiction in telling her story." It could have been made into an exciting, dramatic novel, but then it would have been just another piece of fiction. Her method left the reader with the conviction of absolute authenticity. "You picked up *My Ántonia* to read a novel (love story, of course; hope it's a good one) and find yourself enthralled by autobiography."

As time went on, however, Cather reorganized her memory of the novel's reception. Four years later she had convinced herself that it took the critics two years to discover the book. They didn't like it at first because it had no structure. By 1941 she was writing an old friend that the New York reviewers always lament the fact that her new book (whichever it might be) is a marked decline from the previous one. Logically, she said, she should have reached the vanishing point long ago. She had read practically all the reviews of *My Ántonia* and only two of them from coast to coast were favorable. All the others said the book was formless and would be of interest only to the Nebraska State Historical Society. . . .

Twelve years after the novel appeared, Greenslet sent Justice Oliver Wendell Holmes a copy. The old jurist, then eighty-nine, wrote Greenslet that the book "lifts me to all my superlatives I have not had such a sensation for a long time. To begin with I infinitely respect the author's taking her own environment and not finding it necessary to look for her scenes in Paris or London. I think it a prime mark of a real gift to realize that any piece of the universe may be made poetical if seen by a poet. But to be more concrete, the result seems to me a wonderful success. It has unfailing charm, perhaps not to be defined; a beautiful tenderness, a vivifying imagination that transforms but does not distort or exaggerate—order, proportion." The next year Greenslet sent Holmes *Death Comes for the Archbishop*, and after having his secretary read the novel to him, he wrote Cather directly: "I think you have the gift of the transforming touch. What to another would be prose, under your hand becomes poetry without ceasing to be truth. Among the changes of old age one is that novels are apt to bore me, and I owe you a debt for two exceptions, both of which gave me delight."

Nebraska's Significance for Willa Cather

Doris Grumbach

Given the fact that Willa Cather is credited with making Nebraska a subject worthy of great American literature, it is remarkable that she spent only about twelve years of her life in the state. Nevertheless, Doris Grumbach shows that only through Cather's discovery of Nebraska as material for her short stories and novels did she come into her own as a writer. From out of her familiarity with Nebraska, Cather could, in novels such as *O Pioneers!* and *My Ántonia*, write about what interested her most: the strength of the immigrant women who built lives, farms, and families amid a harsh natural environment. In these apparently unremarkable women rested the enduring values fostered by the land and its attendant hardships. The author of many novels and collections of poems, Doris Grumbach has also been a contributing editor to the *New Republic* and the *New York Times Book Review*. For many years she was a book reviewer for National Public Radio.

It is often assumed that Willa Cather must have been born in Nebraska. . . . But of course this is not true. She was born in 1873 (not 1876) and spent her first nine years in Winchester, Virginia. Hers was an extended family of Boaks and Cathers; she was the first of seven children. Her parents took the family, together with her beloved grandmother, Rachel Boak, and a simple-minded servant, Margie, to the prairie on the Divide and thence, after more than a year, to Red Cloud, Nebraska, because her grandfather, who had gone west earlier, believed it would be a healthier climate for his family.

For Willa, it was psychically a traumatic move. She had loved the lush, damp greenness of the hills and great trees of

Virginia. In Nebraska the child saw flat, hard, tall-grassed land without any signs of human habitation. "I felt a good deal as if we had come to the end of everything," she told an interviewer for the *Philadelphia Record* soon after *O Pioneers!* appeared in 1913. "It was a kind of erasure of personality." She described the new country as "bare as a piece of sheet iron" and admitted: "For the first week or two on the homestead I had the kind of contraction of the stomach which comes from homesickness." Nebraska, she said (through Jim Burden in *My Ántonia*), was "nothing but land: not a country at all, but the material out of which countries are made."

STORIES OF FRONTIER LIFE

Cather received her elementary schooling at home, from her grandmother, and she read to herself from the family's eclectic collection of books. Her enduring education, however, came from her neighbors—Swedish, Danish, Norwegian, and Bohemian (Czech) immigrants—whom she rode out to visit on the bleak prairie. She heard these hardworking people tell the stories of their lives. As she listened, she felt the stirrings of the state in which, years later, she wrote their histories. Later, she told the *Philadelphia Record*, "I used to ride home in the most unreasonable state of excitement: I always felt . . . as if I had actually got inside another person's skin. If one begins that early, it is the story of the man-eating tiger over again—no other adventure ever carries one quite so far."

The stories she heard, the people under whose skins she was able to get, became, in her maturity, her most successful subject matter. She heard about the suicide of Francis Sadilek (father of her friend Annie), the Bohemian farmer who had brought with him from Europe a cultivated love of music. Sadilek despaired of the bleak Nebraska existence and took his life in his barn by shooting himself. This bloody tale stayed with Cather. She must have seen it as a graphic and telling representation of the contradictions in the lives of these immigrants, who were looked down upon for their poverty but were lonely for a culture which was, in many cases, richer than their American neighbors'. She remembered it twice, once in the first story she published, "Peter" (1892), and again, more permanently, as an episode in *My Ántonia.*

Cather also used in her work less dramatic but equally vivid memories of the prairie. The scarceness of trees had impressed her deeply: "Sometimes I went south to visit our German neighbors and to admire their catalpa grove, or to see the big elm tree that grew out of a deep crack in the earth. . . . Trees were so rare in that country . . . that we used to feel anxious about them, and visit them as if they were persons." In *My Ántonia*, a mature Ántonia proudly shows Jim Burden the trees in her orchard: "I love them as if they were people. . . . There wasn't a tree here when we first came." Cather also remembered her grandmother using a walking stick to frighten rattlesnakes away; Jim Burden's grandmother has a "snake-cane." Her own terror of snakes is reflected in some of her books: in *O Pioneers!*, where John Bergson loses his stallion to a snake bite; in *The Song of the Lark*, when Thea warns her brothers of rattlesnakes; in *The Professor's House*, where the story of Henry's death (in two hours) from a rattlesnake is related; and again in *My Ántonia*, where Jim is repulsed by a giant rattler and violently kills it while Ántonia stands by, first screaming and then crying. Years later, Ántonia's and Cuzak's son Charley asks Jim Burden about the rattler he killed at dog-town. . . .

AN UNSUCCESSFUL FIRST NOVEL

In [1911, Cather's] first novel, *Alexander's Bridge*, was accepted and published by Ferris Greenslet at Houghton Mifflin. It is an interesting, if nonpersuasive, international novel in the manner of Henry James. Greenslet heaped praise upon it and, in a memo to other editors in the house, mentioned that it was "workmanlike" and perceptive. Cather herself cared little for this book, belittling it in her preface to the second edition ten years later.

During the summer of 1912 Cather made what turned out to be an important trip to Winslow, Arizona, to vacation with her brother. A section of *The Song of the Lark* draws upon this visit. Thea, in the presence of the silence and mystery of Panther Canyon, makes a crucial decision about her future. I have always assumed that Cather similarly reviewed her life and confirmed her choice of future work; she returned from her trip to Walnut Canyon and the cliff dwellers' ruins even more determined to be a writer of fiction.

Before reaching Arizona, Cather spent the early summer months in Red Cloud. She watched the wheat harvest, a view that renewed her memories of farms and prairie. She had an idea for a story she called "The White Mulberry Tree," about Frank Shabata, a Bohemian farmer, who kills his wife and her lover as they lie under a mulberry tree. Combined with an earlier manuscript she called "Alexandra," it was to be the core of *O Pioneers!* She thought she was on to something good, for she felt a "sense of excitement," she told an interviewer for the *Philadelphia Record* in 1913. The two parts put together, she told her friend Elizabeth Sergeant, were like a "sudden inner explosion and enlightenment." Feeling it, she knew that the form was right, that she had hit upon "the inevitable shape that is not plotted but designed itself." When the book was finished she sent it to Ferris Greenslet, who believed this novel would establish her as a writer of the first rank. It appeared in June 1913 and received exceedingly good reviews.

NEBRASKA BECOMES A UNIVERSAL SETTING

O Pioneers! is a triumph of regional writing given cosmic meaning. Cather must have known that when she wrote to her friend the playwright Zoë Akins: "It was the country that was the hero, or the heroine." It was bigger, greater, than those who peopled and struggled with it. Early in the first section, "The Wild Land," Cather writes. "But the great fact was the land itself, which seemed to overwhelm the little beginnings of human society that struggled in its sombre wastes."

The novel is, properly enough, dedicated to the memory of [author] Sarah Orne Jewett, whose prophecy of knowing the parish Cather was now fulfilling. The epigraph is a 1903 poem of Cather's about the fierce passions of youth and her own feelings for the land. The title of the book is taken from the poem by Walt Whitman: "Through the battle, through defeat, moving yet and never stopping, / Pioneers! O pioneers!" The story is an extraordinary one, episodic and celebratory of the great virtues of heroic persons—like Alexandra Bergson—who hold the land sacred, giving themselves wholly to its dangers and hardships. It begins in pathos with the Swedish girl Alexandra, whose eyes "were fixed intently on the distance," and her little brother, Emil, whose cat is stranded up a pole in the freezing cold of Hanover (Red Cloud under another name), a town "anchored on a windy Nebraska table-land." Young Carl Linstrum enters the story when he rescues the cat and takes the children home. During the long, lyrical account, Alexandra becomes a heroic woman. She is charged by her dying father, who has been defeated by "the wild land he had come to tame," to head the family and to save the land for her brothers and her mother. Cather raises Alexandra to epic status. Driving back with Emil from visiting the rich river farms to assess the farming there, she is triumphant: "Her face was so radiant. . . . For the first time, perhaps, since that land emerged from the waters of geologic ages, a human face was set toward it with love and yearning." This is the glowing prose of epic. The paragraph ends in lofty aphorism: "The history of every country begins in the heart of a man or a woman."

For Alexandra, knowledge of the land is instinctive: "She had not the least spark of cleverness." Her gift is prophetic: "Under the long shaggy ridges, she felt the future stirring."

The novel moves ahead sixteen years. Father and mother have died, the young Bergsons have prospered, the farm is now distinguished by "order and fine arrangement." Alexandra's beloved Emil has grown up, and Carl and his family have given up the struggle and left the land. Then Carl returns for a visit. The two friends resume their talk in rhapsodic terms. She tells him: "It [the land] had its little joke. It pretended to be poor because nobody knew how to work it right; and then, all at once, it worked itself. It woke up out of its sleep and stretched itself." Carl replies that he preferred the way the country was when he was a boy: "There was something about this country when it was a wild old beast that has haunted me all these years."

CATHER FINDS HER TRUE VOICE

Thus, early in her first Nebraska novel, Cather has sounded what are to be major themes in all the immigrant novels: the nobility and beauty of the wild prairie; the brave, enduring foreigners who suffer as they farm it; and the slackness and veniality of the next generation, who inherit the cultivated richness of farms that no longer satisfy them.

Into the pastoral of Alexandra's success enters the tragedy of the love affair of Emil and a neighbor, Marie, and their murder by her wildly jealous husband, Frank. The brave dream has disintegrated. The idealism and innocence of Alexandra ("her mind was a white book, with clear writing about weather and beasts and growing things") have begun to come apart when Carl visits the Bergson brothers; he understands their unworthiness and tells Alexandra: "It is your fate to be always surrounded by little men."

The novel closes with the heartbroken Alexandra as forgiving savior, selflessly promising to help free Frank, who is in jail. Carl returns to claim her in marriage, but on her terms. They will travel but then will come back to the farm to live. Carl, echoing the first chapter's sentimentality, tells her: "You belong to the land. . . . Now more than ever." Alexandra, in her prophetic manner, responds: "The land belongs to the future, Carl; that's the way it seems to me." Their union is not to be romantic or passionate, we know. Alexandra assures him: "When friends marry, they are safe." Cather's summary elegy is contained in the last lines of the novel: "Fortunate country, that is one day to receive hearts like Alexandra's into its bosom, to give them out again in the yellow wheat, in the rustling corn, in the shining eyes of youth!"

The power of *O Pioneers!* lies in Cather's resolve to raise what Ellen Moers in *Literary Women* calls her "empress of the prairie" to the heights of epic proportions. To a cast of characters who are Swedish, "heavy farming people, with cornfields and pasture lands and pig yards, set in Nebraska of all places!" (Cather's description), she gives nobility and eddic enchantment. Alexandra is as creative with the land as are the artists in Cather's earlier stories. She becomes part of a historic dream, conqueror of the forces of nature. The personified land and Alexandra, one with the land, are the stuff of American epic. Nebraska, Cather saw, was not simply territory or one homesteaded place on the American continent, but a universal symbol of suffering and hardship overcome by the indomitable immigrant spirit. . . .

THE FULFILLMENT OF CATHER'S GENIUS

Between the appearance of *The Song of the Lark* and the publication of *My Ántonia* (1918), perhaps Cather's most distinguished novel, a great deal happened. During that period she had some negative feelings about her publishers, who she felt were not promoting *The Song of the Lark* properly. But she was a good friend of Ferris Greenslet's, so her next book, *One of Ours,* would go to Houghton Mifflin. However, after *My Ántonia,* she was to change publishers. The young and enterprising Alfred A. Knopf, she thought, worked hard on behalf of his writers and his concern for the appearance of a book interested her. (The bindings of both *O*

Pioneers! and *My Ántonia* were a rather dull brown.) Cather did not profit much from *The Song of the Lark;* she had to spend some time writing short stories to make money.

Moreover, in 1916 the announcement of the marriage of her beloved friend Isabelle McClung to the Russian-Jewish violinist Jan Hambourg deeply affected her. For almost a year she wrote little. Her friend Elizabeth Sergeant reported Cather's desolation: "Her face—I saw how bleak it was, how vacant her eyes. All her natural exuberance had drained away." Some of her initial turmoil over this marriage was apparently worked off in two stories of the period ("The Diamond Mine" and "Scandal"), both of which contain unpleasant characters who are Jewish. But she soon reconciled herself to the union and in fact became close to Jan Hambourg as well; she would later dedicate *The Professor's House* to him.

Later that winter she vacationed in Taos, a place that was to figure largely in *Death Comes for the Archbishop,* and she stopped off in Nebraska on her way home to New York. She visited Annie Pavelka, her childhood Bohemian friend whose father . . . committed suicide. What she saw most probably became, in *My Ántonia,* Jim Burden's vision of Ántonia married and surrounded by her many children. . . .

THE TIMELESSNESS OF THE LAND

In no other book has Cather invoked the mystic nature of man's relation to the soil so timelessly as in *My Ántonia.* The hired girls are in Black Hawk, Nebraska; once again, Cather has simply renamed Red Cloud. As in *O Pioneers!* the heroine is a woman close to the soil, this time a version of Annie Pavelka ("a Bohemian girl who was good to me when I was a child," Cather wrote), whom she calls Ántonia Shimerda. E.K. Brown, one of Cather's biographers, writes: "It seemed to her [Cather] that this woman's story ran very close to the central stream of life in Red Cloud and on the Divide, that she stood for the triumph of what was vigorous, sound, and beautiful in a region where these qualities so often seemed to suffer repression or defeat." Jim Burden's friend, in the introduction to *My Ántonia,* says, "More than any other person we remembered, this girl seemed to mean to us the country, the conditions, the whole adventure of our childhood."

Cather wrote: "There are only two or three human stories, and they go on repeating themselves as fiercely as if they had never happened before." The story of *My Ántonia* is not in the form of a conventional novel, but more a series of dramatic or elegiac episodes. The excuse for the form is provided by Jim Burden: "I didn't have time to arrange it; I simply wrote down pretty much all that her name recalls to me. I suppose it hasn't any form." Jim is thus released from organizing the material, and the reader learns, haphazardly, of his unhappy marriage and of his job as a railroad lawyer which takes him back and forth across the country, inevitably back to the land of his childhood and to the girl he remembers so romantically. We hear of his boyhood on his grandfather's farm near Black Hawk and of the dirt-poor Czech family he knew, the Shimerdas, immigrants struggling to live on the land they have bought and paid too much for.

The terrifying story of the Russian couple on their bridal trip who are thrown to the wolves from their sled is dropped into the pastoral narrative somewhat irrelevantly. Cather loved artistic contrast, the violent event set against the monotony of life on the prairie. A second violent episode is Mr. Shimerda's suicide, a tragic occurrence that dramatizes the startling antithesis of the hardships endured by the immigrants—drought, frost, grasshoppers, plagues, prairie fires, privation, isolation, loneliness—and the life Mr. Shimerda left behind in Bohemia. There he loved to play the fiddle at dances and weddings. Jim says: "I knew it was homesickness that had killed Mr. Shimerda."

The Burdens move into Black Hawk, and Ántonia comes to town to become a maid (a "hired girl") at the Harlings', as Annie Sadilek did in the home of the Miners, Cather's girlhood friends, to whom the book is dedicated. Ántonia is not easily tamed. Her love of dancing, of which Mrs. Harling disapproves, causes her to give up her job. "A girl like me has got to take her good times when she can," she says. Into this narrative, violent and dramatic anecdotes are dropped––the tramp who jumps into the threshing machine and is cut to pieces, the entry of the blind Negro piano player, and, after Ántonia goes to work for the Cutters, the plan of Wick Cutter to rape her (prevented by Jim). Nowhere in Cather's work are there persons as despicable as the Cutters, whose marriage is childless and loveless. He is a money-lender, a gambler, a womanizer, one of the "fast set," and she is a mean-spirited horror. "I have found Mrs. Cutters all over the world," Cather said later. Over the years, readers of the novel have formed a strong dislike of the Cutters. When the "Cutter House" is pointed out on tours of Red Cloud, Cather pilgrims have been known to hiss loudly at the name.

THE STRENGTH OF THE LAND AND THE
PETTINESS OF BLACK HAWK

Jim Burden dislikes town life and town people: "How much jealousy and envy and unhappiness some of them [the frail houses] managed to contain! The life that went on in them seemed to me made up of evasions and negations. . . ." In this section Cather gives us a memorable symbol of pioneers and landscape, the conquered frontier, that still haunts her readers: "On some upland farm, a plough had been left standing in the field. The sun was sinking just behind it. Magnified across the distance by the horizontal light, it stood out against the sun, was exactly contained within the circle of the disk; the handles, the tongue, the shard—black against the molten red. There it was, heroic in size, a picture writing on the sun."

The story has suddenly shifted (Jim Burden warned us his memories would be poorly ordered) to two other hired girls he admires, Lena Lingard and Tiny Soderball, who are to succeed in later life as a dressmaker and a gold speculator. We learn the details of Jim's student life in Lincoln. Ántonia drops out of the story until Jim hears of her disgrace by the railroad man Larry Donovan, who has left her with an illegitimate child. This traumatic event, which we learn at third hand, brings Ántonia back to the farm where, in the final chapter (Cather customarily brings her story to an end many years after the action of the novel), Jim sees her once again. She is now middle-aged, married to the Czech Anton Cuzak, has many children, and is "battered but not diminished." And what is more, she "[has] not lost the fire of life." Here on the farm all is peace, contentment, and fertility. It is the last picture of the series that composes the book, what E.K. Brown calls a "mournful appreciation" of (in Jim Burden's last words) "the precious, the incommunicable past." The reader thinks back to Jim's reading of Virgil's *Georgics:* "Optima dies . . . prima fugit" (The best days are the first to flee). These rueful words are the book's epigraph, and there is autobiographical truth in the continuation: "Primus ego in patriam mecum . . . deducam Musas" (For I shall be the first, if I live, to bring the Muse into my country). Cather always believed that *My Ántonia* was "the best thing I've ever done . . . I feel I've made a contribution to American letters in that book."

My Ántonia and Immigration on the American Frontier

Sally Allen McNall

America in the late nineteenth century witnessed un-
precedented levels of emigration from central and
eastern Europe, which in turn ignited equally un-
precedented social and political tensions in the United
States. Many solutions were suggested to the problem
of immigration and its perceived effect on America's
Anglo-Saxon identity. Debate over assimilation, cultural pluralism, and unabashed xenophobia (suspicion and hostility toward all foreigners) was as heated
in the 1890s as it is today. In the following excerpt,
Sally Allen McNall illustrates how deeply My Ántonia
confronts the issue of immigration and American
identity. Through Cather's subtle portrayal of hierar-
chies among the immigrants on the frontier, her
treatment of Catholicism, and the fears the townspeople of Black Hawk harbor toward the "hired
girls," the reader is given deep insight into the trials
of settlement and community making on the American frontier. Sally Allen McNall has taught American
literature at the University of Arizona and the University of Kansas. She is the author of *Who Is in the
House?: A Psychological Study of Two Centuries of
Women's Fiction in America* (1981).

My Ántonia is about the historical period during which the
American frontier closed. It is also about the place where that
happened, since the Great Plains were settled after the West
Coast regions; the people of the Great Plains, more than those
of any other region, must be thought of as immigrants. In the
nineties, the historian Frederick Jackson Turner began to ex-

Excerpted from Sally Allen McNall, "Immigrant Backgrounds to *My Ántonia:* 'A Curious Social Situation in Black Hawk,'" in *Approaches to Teaching Cather's* My Ántonia,
edited by Susan Rosowski. Reprinted with permission from the Modern Language Association of America.

pound his thesis explaining the American character in terms of the frontier. In shifting emphasis from the East to the "Great West," he also developed an idea of the frontier as a crucible, where European immigrants were "Americanized, liberated, and fused into a mixed race." The idea of the West as melting pot was appealing in the years before World War I, but it was only one way in which Americans could think about immigrants. Three years before *My Ántonia* was published, the *Nation* printed an influential article presenting another view. According to the philosopher H.M. Kallen, each nationality should express its "emotional and voluntary life in its own language, in its own inevitable aesthetic and intellectual forms." This currently popular idea has since been termed cultural pluralism and recently, by Carl Degler, the "salad bowl." There is no doubt that it appealed to Cather as strongly as Turner's frontier thesis could have done. Her attitude toward the immigrant is partly a matter of deeply personal identification with those who are "different," but it also may reflect Nebraska's relative noninterference with various ethnic lifestyles, compared with its Great Plains neighbors.

ASSIMILATION, NATIVISM, AND XENOPHOBIA

A first reading of *My Ántonia*, when it was originally published, in 1918, or today, may leave a reader with the impression of either a melting pot or a salad bowl. In "Cuzak's Boys" the respectability of town (the teachings of Mrs. Burden and Mrs. Harling) and the cosmopolitanism of city (Cuzak's background) support Ántonia's role as a "rich mine of life," founding not an old but a new race: Americans, with a living cultural heritage from the Old World. Yet an examination of the book as a whole, in the context of some far less benign theories and myths, will show students that Cather was equally aware of the other side of her cultural coinage.

In its most acceptable form, the earliest theory of "Americanization" can be called assimilation. In Cather's day it deserved the description "doctrine of Anglo-Saxon conformity," and it was a widespread response to the influx of immigration between 1880 and 1914. The years—1883 to 1895—when Cather lived in Nebraska neatly span the middle portion of the two decades during which the national question of immigration become more vexed than ever before in our history. In those decades and the two to follow, the rigid classification of social identities in the United States reached its peak. Nativism, as it was called, had been present from the beginning of the century of immigration (roughly, 1820–1920). In a society always profoundly subject to change, xenophobia was an early and persistent response to insecurity, and in the 1890s Americans were particularly insecure economically. Although immigration to the Great Plains slowed during this decade, immigration on a national level did not; in fact, xenophobia was probably exacerbated by the condition of the numerous urban immigrants. Nativism infected all sections of the country and every class, but it was not new. "If I were to put upon the printed page some of the epithets applied to . . . people from central Europe . . . by their prairie and backwoods neighbors, in the seventies and eighties," observes a Nebraska educator in 1929, "I greatly fear it would not add to the growing cordiality between this group and the rest of us."

The growing movement for regulation of immigration argued that the arrival of cheap foreign labor was not only undesirable competition but a contribution to the widening and hardening gap between rich and poor. Not only labor unrest in cities but the agrarian protest movements Cather knew well were regularly blamed on foreign radicals. Students should know that between 1895 and the publication of *My Ántonia,* Cather lived in Pittsburgh and (like the "I" of the introduction) in New York City, where the conditions of urban immigrants could hardly be ignored and where—as newspaperwoman and editor for a radical magazine, *McClure's*—Cather was exposed to a variety of facts and opinions on the subject.

IMMIGRANT HIERARCHIES IN *MY ÁNTONIA*

During those years, yet another way of viewing immigrants was developing. Immigrants had begun to reach the Great Plains within the decade after the Homestead Act (1862). During that decade and in the seventies, immigrants to America were predominantly from western and northern Europe. Though the promotional activities of the railroads now brought many straight past the cities of the East to the prairies, other immigrants were moving on from earlier settlements in the East. In *My Ántonia,* the Harlings, Mrs. Gardener (née Molly Bawn), and Mr. Jensen, the Danish laundryman, are examples of this group, soon to be called the "old immigrants." These people were more easily integrated into our society than were the "new immigrants" from eastern and southern Europe, whose numbers swelled in the eighties and nineties. The Harlings, in particular, illustrate the proposition that Scandinavian immigrants tended to be upright and cosmopolitan, while Lena Lingard's grandfather was a "clergyman and much respected in Norway." Despite a dubious reputation, Lena does not get in trouble; rather, she is a success American-style, as is Tiny Soderball. Though many Czechs arrived in Nebraska at the same time as the western and northern Europeans, the national picture was different, and the Shimerdas reflect this change, arriving late, on the largest wave of Czech immigration.

By the 1890s, Italians, eastern European Jews, and Slavs (a group that includes Czechs) were arriving in great numbers, and they bore the brunt of the economic insecurity of the period. During the years Cather was writing *My Ántonia,* America was making up its mind whether to go to war with Germany and Austria-Hungary. Czechs in America were eager even before our involvement to help free their homelands from the domination of the Dual Empire; early in the book Otto makes an elliptical reference to the background of this situation. Yet Czechs like other immigrants felt the force of the Americanization movement in the war years, while Germans in America, including Nebraska, were definitely suspect; stories of their victimization can be found in almost any history of a midwestern state. The country's anxiety over the role immigrants were to play in our society did not ease, though the "tide" of immigration was stemmed, briefly, by the war; after the war years, the restrictionists won their battles, in the quota system—based on the preexisting composition of the American population—instituted in 1921 and 1924. The "new" immigrants, then, were regarded with suspicion, which took several forms, each revealing fears about American institutions. Cather misses none of them.

The most prominent anxiety in "The Hired Girls" is sexual—it concerns marriage. It is no accident that the dancing pavilion that menaces the morals of Black Hawk youth is set up by an Italian couple. Black Hawk attitudes are polarized by the dances along the lines between "old" and "new" immigrant stereotypes—the Danish laundry girls contrasted with the dangerous Bohemian Marys, and Ántonia's success at the tent the first step toward her downfall.

Students may not be aware how xenophobia in America fed, from the beginning, on a set of ideas that can only be termed racist, ideas about "mongrelization," and Anglo-

Saxons' being "outbred" by inferior racial groups, ideas of a "dark shadow" or a "black tide." The "new" immigrants were seen as more peasantlike than the "old"; a thread of this sort of distaste on the part of the Burdens runs through "The Shimerdas." Jim reacts with violent self-righteousness to unpleasant facts concerning Ántonia's sexuality: the rape, the first pregnancy. His reactions here ironically prefigure the way he will repeat Sylvester Lovett's pattern, will toy with Lena but marry a wealthy bloodless woman of his own ethnicity and class.

Sexuality, then, threatens both the "racial purity" and the respectability of old Black Hawk residents. It is also a threat to the immigrant, and here Cather takes considerable pains to make her point clear. In Ántonia, she creates a character whose moral isolation is all but total, who must do without the support of extended family and tradition, who must rely on herself alone to make her marital arrangements, and who at first fails disastrously. In the Old World, she would have lived, as virtually all Czech immigrants had, in a village community and would have been courted by someone like Cuzak to begin with. The absence of community is destructive to her as well as to her father. If they had come to eastern Nebraska, they would have benefited from the colony-based settlement system; Webster County's settlements were never large. No one is there to understand, much less sympathize with, peasant values; to the Burdens, she seems degraded by her work. Ántonia's status is precarious, then, long before the dance pavilion comes to Black Hawk, and afterward it is clear that she is regarded as "fair game," not only by Wick Cutter but, in his unconscious way, by Jim, who kisses her in a manner that is "not right."

Toward the end of "The Hired Girls," an important passage tells us about the class split in Ántonia's background. Her father "lived in his mother's house," says Ántonia to Jim, and she [Ántonia's mother] was a poor girl come in to do the work." Ántonia is the daughter of a servant who was no better than she should be, a stereotype of the undesirable immigrant, and temporarily at least Ántonia too fulfills that role.

RELIGIOUS TENSIONS IN *MY ÁNTONIA*

Another influence that bound many Bohemians of Ántonia's generation into a community and preserved traditional values for more than one or two generations is all but absent from

Cather's picture of the character. Bohemian immigrants, like many others, often settled in communities built around their churches, particularly in the Midwest and West. Today's students are generally surprised to learn that a powerful current in American xenophobia, from the days of the Puritans, was a horror of the Roman Catholic church. The Shimerdas (like approximately fifty percent of all Czech immigrants) are Catholic. In the 1890s, American fear of domination or at least subversion by those loyal to a foreign potentate, the pope, and fear of a religious tradition not particularly interested in the cause of temperance were aggravated by conflicts in the East and Midwest over the issue of parochial schools, where classes were often taught in the children's native languages, and which, unlike our public schools, did not "Americanize."

Twice in *My Ántonia,* Cather—most uncharacteristically—emphasizes elements of Catholicism that were, in the eyes of contemporary American Protestants, mere popish superstition. The scenes in question are Mr. Shimerda's spontaneous prayer before the Christmas tree—which Grandfather Burden "Protestantizes"—and Mrs. Shimerda's desire to bury her husband, a suicide and hence a mortal sinner, at a crossroads. This desire is frustrated by later (one assumes Protestant) road makers. Cather presents Ántonia and her family as isolates, lacking a stable and coherent religious community and tradition, and therefore the sort of religious ties that could prevent the mistake she makes with Larry Donovan. Yet if the reputable Protestants of Black Hawk participated in the anti-Catholic prejudice of their times, a Catholic girl's fall (and with a Catholic young man) would not have surprised them.

EDUCATION AND THE "MELTING POT" OF AMERICA

Although Antonia has no religious training to help her preserve her Czech identity, she is at any rate spared the "Americanization" of the public schools. If our students take the value of public education for granted, they need to be reminded that immigrants did not invariably do so. As another member of Cather's generation in Nebraska observed of his Czech pupils, their families "wanted the children to get an English education, but corn husking took precedence over everything." In a 1923 *Nation* article, Cather comments tartly that our lawmakers "have a rooted conviction that a boy can be a better American if he speaks only one language than if he speaks two." It is not necessarily Ántonia's loss that she has no time for school, and it is part of her triumph that her children grow up bilingual, speaking Czech at home and preserving Czech ways.

Ántonia's father's plea, "Te-e-ach, te-e-ach my Ántonia!" is that of an educated man helpless to pass his education on to the child who takes after him; it is not a wish that her mind should be molded to that of the New World. Cather points out that "Many of our Czech immigrants were people of a very superior type. The political emigration resulting from the revolutionary disturbances of 1848 was distinctly different from the emigration resulting from economic causes . . . in Nebraska our Czech settlements were large and very prosperous." Many such settlements in fact resulted from internal migration from early Czech colonies in Wisconsin and Ohio, but this clustering argues for a considerable degree of difference perceived between the Czechs and the dominant culture, and of course the Shimerdas, however superior a type Mr. Shimerda was, do not have the advantage of living in a large settlement.

For Jim, obviously, education—especially higher education—is an important indicator of class and a means of upward mobility. The relative lack of education of the "new" immigrants was one reason nativists gave for fearing them. Ántonia never gets a formal education, nor is she upwardly mobile; rather, she stays put—a "country girl." Students may need to be told that by the time described in "Cuzak's Boys," farming—however prosperous—had lost the prestige it had had in America since Jefferson's day. Class and immigrant status were intertwined, even in rural Nebraska.

THE PAIN OF ADAPTING TO FRONTIER LIFE

In a rapidly industrializing and urbanizing America, economic dislocations between generations were inevitable, particularly for immigrant families who went to cities, but also in rural life. Mr. Shimerda is not the sort of man who can adapt to frontier conditions. As Annie Sadilek Pavelka put it in a 1955 letter, her father, a weaver in the old country, was totally unprepared for the prairies:

> he used to hear how good it was hear as he had letters from her how wonderfull it was out here that there were beautiffull houses lot of trees and so on but how disapointed he was when he saw them pretty houses duged in the banks of the deep draws . . . behold our surprise . . . in the old country he was allways joking and happy.

Many Bohemian villagers with crafts found them of little use in the agricultural environment. In Cather's novel, however, Ántonia and also her brother can and do adapt to the prairie. Cuzak, Ántonia's husband, knew little about farming to begin with, but Ántonia's strength, and the children, have made the difference. "We got plenty boys," he says (chilling any Anglo-Saxon supremacist), "we can work a lot of land." This is traditional farming, and Cather has Jim look back on the stories of the immigrant girls in a way that maintains a distinction between farming and business. "Today," Jim says, "the best that a harassed Black Hawk merchant can hope for is to sell provisions and farm machinery and automobiles to the rich farms where that first crop of stalwart Bohemian and Scandinavian girls are now mistresses."

Cather's vision of immigrants to central Nebraska in the crucial years retains much of the uglier furniture of the American mind at the time. Over Jim's head we see—and, with Cather, may judge—the ethnocentricity permeating every social institution. The harshness of this reality is mitigated by Jim's bemused sporadic attraction to Ántonia's very foreignness. But Ántonia is just that: Jim's romantic heroine. As Frances Harling tells him, "I expect I know the country girls better than you do. You always put a kind of glamour over them. The trouble with you, Jim, is that you're romantic." Because Jim's own life, marriage, and work involve him inextricably in the world of business, as we learn in the introduction, he cannot see the contradictions in the rural lives he idealizes. Cather can, and she even has Ántonia warn Jim as a boy of his blindness: "Things will be easy for you. But they will be hard for us."

RESISTANCE TO AMERICAN PUBLIC OPINION OF IMMIGRANTS

While she wrote *My Ántonia*, Cather was as aware of the climate of opinion, the emphasis on being one hundred percent American, as was any major writer of her time. She wrote against universal conformity, without polemic and without oversimplification. In a world in which foreignness was the symbol of insecurity and change, she made an immigrant woman stand for permanence and stability. This trick is not the only one she played. In "Nebraska: The End of the First Cycle," she deplored the "machine-made materialism" that industrialization was producing. Because she confronts this issue head-on in her 1922 novel *One of Ours*, it is tempting, and certainly easier on our students, to teach *My Ántonia* as a looking back to a time and way of life uncontaminated by materialism, by capitalistic development and its imperatives. For both Jim and the narrator of the introduction, Ántonia means "the country, the conditions, the whole adventure of our childhood." Jim's vision of an immigrant woman triumphing over adversity does indeed look back, but Cather's vision, I try to show my students, examines the social conflicts beneath the mythologies of her day, looks far enough into them to suggest powerfully what our imported labor force was up against in her day.

It is still up against it today. We have not yet made up our minds what we want to do about or with immigrants. Because of this, *My Ántonia* remains a central text in our literature and can heighten our students' awareness of the history of their mythologies and attitudes.

CHAPTER 2

My Ántonia's Structure, Setting, and Themes

READINGS ON
MY ÁNTONIA

The Structure of
My Ántonia

James E. Miller Jr.

Responding to criticism that *My Ántonia* is full of structural flaws that compromise the novel's success, James E. Miller Jr. defends the novel as subtly structured around the emotions Ántonia engenders in Jim, the cycles of the seasons, and the defining stages of an individual life. Moreover, Miller maintains, the great historical event that frames the novel—the transformation of the American frontier from wilderness into farms and communities—lends a deeper order and significance to the lives of Jim, Ántonia, and the town of Black Hawk. Thus the cycles of nature and the linear progression of historical events that hold the novel together have always appealed to readers, if not to critics. A professor of English at the University of Chicago, James E. Miller Jr. is also a renowned Whitman scholar; his works include Leaves of Grass: *America's Lyric-epic of Self and Democracy* (1992) and *The American Quest for a Supreme Fiction: Walt Whitman's Legacy in the Personal Epic* (1979).

Critics of Willa Cather have long been confronted with the baffling persistence in popularity of a novel apparently defective in structure. *My Ántonia* may well turn out to be Willa Cather's most fondly remembered and best loved novel, while the perfectly shaped, brilliantly executed *A Lost Lady* continues unread. It does seem strange that one who wanted to unclutter the novel by throwing the furniture out the window should have bungled so badly the structure of one of her most important works.

[Critic] René Rapin blames Cather for transplanting Ántonia from the country to Black Hawk: "only in her own nat-

Excerpted from James E. Miller Jr., "*My Ántonia*: A Frontier Drama of Time," *American Quarterly*, 10:4, Winter 1958. Reprinted with permission from the author.

ural habitat can she hold our attention and capture our emotion." And Rapin censures Cather severely for losing sight of Ántonia completely in the closing books of the novel. [Critic] David Daiches discovers the source of the defect in Cather's point of view. The "narrator's sensibility," he says, "takes control; and this raises problems which Willa Cather is never quite able to solve." Like Daiches, [Cather biographer] E.K. Brown is disturbed by the disappearance of Ántonia for pages at a time, and says in the novel's defense: "Everything in the book is there to convey a feeling, not to tell a story, not to establish a social philosophy, not even to animate a group of characters."

Most critics, like Brown, have felt the unified emotional impact of *My Ántonia* and have grappled with the puzzling problem of the book's actual lack of consistent central action or unbroken character portrayal. It is indeed a fine creative achievement to give the effect of unity when there apparently is none, and there are those who would claim that the nature of Cather's accomplishment is beyond the critic's understanding, an inscrutable mystery of the artist's miraculous creative process.

The action in *My Ántonia* is episodic, lacks focus and abounds in irrelevancies (consider the inserted wolf-story of Pavel and Peter, for example). Indeed, there is in the novel no plot in the accepted sense of the word. And further, there is not, as there usually is in the plotless story, a character who remains consistently on stage to dominate the obscurely related events. In the second and third books, entitled respectively "The Hired Girls" and "Lena Lingard," Ántonia fades gradually but completely from view, and the reader becomes engrossed, finally, in the excitingly sensual but abortive relationship of the narrator, Jim Burden, and the voluptuous hired girl turned seamstress, Lena Lingard.

A QUALITY OF FEELING

But there is that quality of evoked feeling which penetrates the pages of the book, inhering even in the scenes omitting Ántonia, and which gathers finally to a profound and singular focus which constitutes the emotional unity of the book. We sense what we cannot detect—structural elements subtly at work reinforcing and sharpening the aroused feeling.

Jim Burden's assertion in the "Introduction" that he supposes the manuscript he has written "hasn't any form"

should not deceive the reader too readily. He also states of
Ántonia, "I simply wrote down pretty much all that her
name recalls to me." If these confessions reveal that neither
action nor character gives unity to the novel, they also suggest, indirectly, that a feeling—the emotion attached to
Ántonia's name—informs the novel structurally. When Jim
Burden, dissatisfied with "Ántonia" as his title, prefixes the
"My," he is informing the reader in advance that the book is
not about the real Ántonia, but rather about Ántonia as personal and poignant symbol. For Jim, Antonia becomes symbolic of the undeviating cyclic nature of all life: Ántonia is
the insistent reminder that it is the tragic nature of time to
bring life to fruition through hardship and struggle only to
precipitate the decline and, ultimately, death, but not without first making significant provision for new life to follow,
flower and fall. The poignancy lies in the inability of the frail
human being to rescue and retain any stage, no matter how
beautiful or blissful, of his precious cycle. When Jim Burden
asserts at the close of *My Ántonia* that he and Ántonia "possess" the "incommunicable past," he does not convince even
himself. It is precisely this emotional conviction that neither
they nor anyone else can possess the past, that the past is absolutely and irrevocably "incommunicable" even to those
who lived it—which constitutes the novel's unity.

The "feeling" of *My Ántonia* is not the divorced and remote and discomforting "feeling" of the author, nor the dis-
played or dramatized "feeling" of a character, but the evoked
feeling of the reader. And the element in the novel which
produces and controls this feeling exists in the sensibility of
the narrator, Jim Burden. It is in the drama of his awakening consciousness, of his growing awareness, that the emotional structure of the novel may be discovered.

THE DRAMA OF THE SEASONS

It is Jim Burden's sensibility which imposes form on *My
Ántonia* and, by that form, shapes in the reader a sharpened
awareness of cyclic fate that is the human destiny. The sense
of cyclic fate finds expression first in an obsessive engagement with the colorful, somber and varied seasons of the
year, next in an unfolding realization of the immutable and
successive phases of human life, and, finally, in an engross-
ing but bewildering encounter with the hierarchic stages of
civilization, from the primitive culture to the sophisticated.

"The Shimerdas," the first book of *My Ántonia*, introduces from the start the drama of time in the vivid accounts of the shifting seasons. The book encompasses one year, beginning with the arrival in Autumn of the Shimerdas and Jim Burden on the endless Nebraska prairie, portraying the terrible struggle for mere existence in the bleakness of the plains' Winter, dramatizing the return of life with the arrival of Spring, and concluding with the promise of rich harvest in the intense heat of the prairie's Summer. This is Jim Burden's remembered year, and it is his obsession with the cycle of time that has caused him to recall Ántonia in a setting of the changing seasons.

Almost every detail in "The Shimerdas" is calculated to shrink the significance of the human drama in contrast with the drama of the seasons, the drama of nature, the drama of the land and sky. The struggle becomes, then, not merely a struggle for a minimum subsistence from the stubborn, foreign soil, but also even more a struggle to re-create and assert existence in a seemingly hostile or indifferent land. No doubt all of the Nebraska pioneers experienced Jim Burden's sensation on arriving on the prairie: "Between that earth and that sky I felt erased, blotted out."

The drama of "The Shimerdas" is the drama of the human being at the mercy of the cyclic nature of the universe. The "glorious autumn" of their arrival on the treeless prairie contributes to that acute sense that "the world was left behind" and that they "had got over the edge of it." The autumn is not the autumn of bountiful nature but the autumn of vast distances and approaching death. The descent of the winter snows heightens the vast primitive beauty of the undisturbed plains: "The sky was brilliantly blue, and the sunlight on the glittering white stretches of prairie was almost blinding." But even innate to the sharp-colored beauty is an apparent hostility. The whiteness not only blinds but brings in its wake despair and death. When, after the first primitive struggle is over, Ántonia cries out to Jim in the midst of summer, "I wish my papa live to see this summer. I wish no winter ever come again," she displays intuitive insight into the relation of her father's suicide to the cosmic order of time which decrees that the death of winter must unfailingly follow the ripening autumn.

Like autumn, spring when it comes to the prairie is not so much manifest in visible nature as it is a hovering presence compellingly alive and dominant: "There was only—spring itself; the throb of it, the light restlessness, the vital essence of it everywhere: in the sky, in the swift clouds, in the pale sunshine, and in the warm, high wind." It is only with the arrival of spring, at its appointed time, that the Shimerdas and the Burdens, Ántonia and Jim, can emerge from the enforced retreat of winter to look forward to some benevolence from the enduring land. But as the winter shaped, and even took, the life of the prairie pioneer, so the spring imposes a cruelly exacting ritual of tilling and tending the virgin land. Life is hard and the soil close and unyielding without its due. And the "breathless, brilliant heat" of summer, when it descends with fiery fury on the empty lands, brings with its devastation also fertility: "The burning sun of those few weeks, with occasional rains at night, secured the corn."

Throughout the first book of *My Ántonia*, it is the world of nature rather than the human world which dominates, and even the human beings tend to identify themselves with the things of the land. One of Jim Burden's first vivid sensations in the new land is in his grandmother's garden: "I was something that lay under the sun and felt it, like the pumpkins, and I did not want to be anything more. I was entirely happy." During their first year on the prairie the rotation of the decreed seasons imposes a primitive existence not far different from that of the plains' animals, and impresses on the pioneers a keenly felt truth: "In a new country a body feels friendly to the animals." If in the garden Jim imagined himself a pumpkin, there were other times when he and the rest felt a sympathetic resemblance to the gopher, in their intimate dependence on the land for sustenance and home. At the end of this first year's struggle with the land, Ántonia emerges with an essential and profound wisdom that only the cyclic seasons in their cruelty and their beneficence could bestow. She reveals to Jim, "Things . . . will be hard for us."

As Ántonia and Jim are shaped and "created" by the successive seasons, so their lives in turn are cycles of a larger order in time, and shape and create the nation. It is in the dramatization of Ántonia from the girlhood of the opening pages through her physical flowering in the middle books to, finally, her reproduction of the race in a flock of fine boys in the final pages of the book that her life is represented, like the year with its seasons, as a cycle complete in its stages of birth, growth, fruition and decline. Although Ántonia's life represents a greater cycle than that of the year, the pattern remains the same in both. The year, of course, is merely a term for the designation of a unit of time, and its resemblance to the life-cycle suggests that life, too, is a physical representation of time.

THE STAGES OF ÁNTONIA'S LIFE

As the seasons of fall, winter, spring and summer impose a structure on the first book of Willa Cather's novel, the successive stages of Ántonia's life assist in imposing a structure on the total work. We may trace these stages through the various books into which the novel is subdivided. Some critics have called Ántonia an earth goddess. She is a re-creation of an archetypal pattern—woman as the embodiment of self-assured if not self-contained physical fertility which insures the endurance of the race. Ántonia never despairs, not even in the first book of the novel in which the hostility of the first prairie winter deprives her of her father; but throughout she works and lives with an innate dignity which springs from her intuitive knowledge of her appointed function in the continuation of the species. Even in the second book, called "The Hired Girls," Ántonia feels no sense of an enforced inferiority but rather a supreme reliance on the hidden resources bestowed upon her by the hard physical struggles of her past.

As Ántonia stands out sharply in the first book, in the second she merges with many "hired girls" in Black Hawk who are of her kind, and in the third, called "Lena Lingard," she does not even appear except as a remembered presence in the talks about the past between Lena and Jim Burden in Lincoln. In these conversations there is a foreshadowing of Ántonia's fate which is the subject of the fourth book, entitled "The Pioneer Woman's Story." If in Book I Ántonia represents the eternal endurance under supreme hardship of woman appointed propagator of the race, and in Book II she represents the overflowing liveliness and energetic abundance of physical woman come to the flower, in Books III and IV she symbolizes the calm and faithful endurance of woman eternally wronged. In Ántonia's fierce love for her fatherless child exists the full explanation of mankind's continuing to be. But Willa Cather insists on Ántonia's appearing in a double role, not only as woman wronged, but also as woman fulfilled in her destiny. In the last book of the novel, "Cuzak's Boys," Ántonia is glimpsed in her declining years surrounded by the "explosive life" of her many children. When Jim Burden sees her after the absence of all those years, he recognizes in her the persistence of that quality he had sensed when they roamed the prairie as boy and girl: "She was there, in the full vigour of her personality, battered but not diminished, looking at me, speaking to me in the husky, breathy voice I remembered so well."

MY *ÁNTONIA* AND THE EVOLUTION OF FRONTIER SETTLEMENT

In the closing books of *My Ántonia* ("The Pioneer Woman's Story" and "Cuzak's Boys"), Ántonia emerges as vividly as she did in the first. For an explanation of the fading of Ántonia in Books II and III ("The Hired Girls" and "Lena Lingard"), we must turn to a third principle of structure operating in the book, another cycle greater in scope than either a year or a life. For a foreshadowing of this cycle we may turn to Frederick Jackson Turner and his famous essay, "The Significance of the Frontier in American History." Turner asserted, in the late nineteenth century, that the distinguishing feature of America's development was the cyclic character of her movement westward, conquering over and over again a new wilderness. There was, Turner said, "a recurrence of the process of evolution in each western area reached in the process of expansion."

My Ántonia exemplifies superbly Turner's concept of the recurring cultural evolution on the frontier. There is first of all the migration from the East, in the case of the Shimerdas from Czechoslovakia, in Jim Burden's case from Virginia, both lands of a high cultural level. In the West these comparatively sophisticated people are compelled literally to begin over again, on a primitive level, shedding their cultural attainment like an animal its skin, and, like animals, doing battle with the land and the elements for the meanest food and shelter.

The books of *My Ántonia* reflect the varying stages of this evolutionary process in cultural development. On this level of structure, not the seasons of the year, nor the phases of Ántonia's life, but the successive cultural plateaus of the nation operate as ordering elements in the novel. And it is on this level of significance and in the dramatization of this epic archetypal cycle of the country that justification for those sections of the book, so frequently condemned because they lose focus on Ántonia, may be found.

In the first book, "The Shimerdas," the newly arrived pioneers from the East discover nothing but their strength and the prairie's stubborn soil out of which to create for themselves a new world in their own image. In this primitive struggle with the prairie, on a level with the struggle of prehistoric man in the dawn of time, some lose their lives, some their spirit, and all lose that overlay of softening civilization which they brought from the East. There is not only the primitive struggle, but these pioneers become primitive men in the harshness of the struggle. Ántonia's father, sad for the old country, dies; and Ántonia takes a man's place behind the plow. On the prairie the elements, the sky and the land impose a communal democracy in all of the meager human institutions.

"The Hired Girls," the second book of *My Ántonia,* portrays a higher stage in the cultural evolution of the frontier: the small town comes to the wilderness. If Jim Burden discovers his own hidden courage and becomes a man in the snake-killing incident of Book I, in Book II he discovers the genuine complexity of adulthood, especially in a social context which the bare prairie does not afford. Jim is puzzled by the stratification of society in Black Hawk, a stratification that could not exist on the virgin prairie, and which does not tally with Jim's moral judgment: the "hired girls" are for Jim the most interesting, the most exciting and the liveliest of all possible companions, far superior to the dull conformists of the town. It is the strong lure of the hired girls, however, which precipitates Jim's first crucial decision: in spite of the strong spiritual and physical attraction of these girls, Jim turns to the study which will prepare him for college and which, in Black Hawk, culminates in the triumph of his high school commencement oration. Already there has come to the frontier prairie that element whose absence caused Ántonia's father to despair. After Ántonia has heard Jim's speech, she tells him: "there was something in your speech that made me think so about my papa." In her instinctive way Ántonia dimly understands her father's sacrifice of his life and Jim's yearning for higher intellectual achievement, even though her own destiny, centered in the physical reproduction of the race, may be and is to be fulfilled on the innocent and unsophisticated prairie.

Jim's discoveries, both intellectual and emotional, of Book II, are continued and intensified in the next book, "Lena Lingard." Lincoln, Nebraska, is as far above Black Hawk culturally as Black Hawk is above the empty, untouched prairie, and though the university has the limitations imposed by the isolation of the plains, there is "an atmosphere of endeavour, of expectancy and bright hopefulness" which prevails. It is Jim's good fortune to develop a close association with Gaston Cleric, the intellectually alive and intense head of the Latin Department, who introduces Jim to the exciting world of ideas. Jim discovers that "when one first enters that world everything else fades for a time, and all that went before is as if it had not been." But the climax of Jim's awakening is a realization of the persistence of the past: "Yet I found curious survivals; some of the figures of my old life seemed to be waiting for me in the new." Jim's awareness of the crucial impingement of his prairie heritage on his involvement in a received culture seems an instinctive artistic confirmation of Turner's frontier thesis.

Culture does come to the Nebraska prairie, not only in the form of a world of ideas via Gaston Cleric, but also in the form of music and theater. The nature of the curious impact is revealed brilliantly when Jim describes his and Lena's reaction to the traveling "Camille": "A couple of jackrabbits, run in off the prairie, could not have been more innocent of what awaited them." Throughout Book III of the novel, there is a delightful rediscovery by the children of the pioneer generation of a cultural world forsaken by their parents for the hard and isolated life of the prairie. But the pioneer values of freshness and courage and integrity—and many more—survive and condition the responses.

THE CYCLE OF CULTURAL MOVEMENT

Lincoln, Nebraska, though it offers much, offers a mere token of what waits in the rich and glittering East. Lured on by bright dreams of intellectual achievement, Jim Burden follows Gaston Cleric to Harvard, which, in the book's developing hierarchy, is to Lincoln as Lincoln is to Black Hawk and Black Hawk to the barren prairie. But with the dramatization of three stages of civilization as it comes to the wilderness, and with the suggestion of the future destiny by the "invocation" of "ancient" Harvard and by the suggestion of greater cultural riches farther East, Willa Cather shifts the

focus from the dream of the nation and, indeed, of civilization, back to Ántonia of the prairies. The novel has, in a
sense, come full circle when Jim, in the last book, finds himself in the midst of that very culture the nostalgic remembrance of which drove Ántonia's father to despair: "Once
when I was abroad I went into Bohemia, and from Prague I
sent Ántonia some photographs of her native village." By
this casual visit, the return to the point of origin, the cycle of
cultural movement is symbolically completed. And when
the sophisticated, world-traveled, perhaps even world-
weary, Jim Burden returns to the prairie scenes of his boyhood and discovers Ántonia and her houseful of boys, he discovers at the same time the enduring quality of those values
not dependent on cultural level, but accessible on the untu-
tored prairies. Ántonia, "in the full vigour of her personality,
battered but not diminished," not only endures but achieves
an emotionally and physically fulfilled life. Her boys are her
triumphant creative achievement.

My Ántonia closes with the dominant image of the circle,
a significant reminder of the general movement of all the
structural elements in the book. After his visit with Ántonia,
Jim confesses, "I had the sense of coming home to myself,
and of having found out what a little circle man's experience
is." This vivid image reinforces the cyclic theme which pervades the book: the cycle of the seasons of the year, the cycle of the stages of human life, the cycle of the cultural
phases of civilization. *My Ántonia* is, then, ultimately about
time, about the inexorable movement of future into present,
of present into past. Against the backdrop of this epic drama
of the repetitive movement of time, man poignantly plays out
his role. Ántonia, when she cries out to Jim, "I wish no winter ever come again," more nearly expresses the essence of
the book's theme than does Jim when he asserts at the end,
"whatever we had missed, we possessed together the precious, the incommunicable past." *Optima dies . . . prima
fugit*, translated by Jim as "the best days are the first to flee,"
stands as the book's epigraph. This intensely felt awareness
of the past *as past* is the emotional heart of the novel, and is
evoked and sustained by the book's several levels of structure and their involvement with the revolving cycles of time.

An American Pastoral

David Stouck

In its simplest form, the pastoral represents an escape
into a highly idealized celebration of rural simplicity
and innocence. As a literary genre, it originates in the
poetry and drama of the ancient Greeks, and has appeared in Western literature in one form or another
ever since. In *My Ántonia*, the pastoral is located on
the Nebraska plains, and we find its themes of innocence and a carefree spirit in Jim's desire to recover
the apparently timeless life he lived as a youth in the
company of Ántonia. Yet David Stouck notes that,
true to American representations of the pastoral,
Jim's desire to ground himself in his memories of innocence and a sense of timelessness is undermined.
Cather makes it clear to the reader that Jim's ideals
cannot possibly be fulfilled, and that the past can
never be recovered. For Stouck, the tension between
Jim's idealizations of his childhood, the loss of innocence that adulthood entails, and Jim's need to imaginatively affirm his rural past invigorates and informs the structure of *My Ántonia*. David Stouck
teaches English at Simon Fraser University in Van-
couver, British Columbia.

In every work of art there exists a fundamental tension between two irreconcilable motives, for art has its source and
momentum in conflict that cannot be resolved. A straightforward example is *Huckleberry Finn*, where the vernacular
style returns us nostalgically to childhood and at the same
time establishes a naive viewpoint for satire—Mark Twain
being torn between a sentimental and a vicious view of the
past. Similarly, in [F. Scott Fitzgerald's] *The Great Gatsby* the
romantic vision of Gatsby is continuously undercut by the

ironic viewpoint of the narrator, Nick Carraway. The style in these novels is double-edged, embodying the author's conflicting emotions. The nondramatic style of *My Ántonia* makes the idea of conflict seem of little relevance to the novel, but pastoral art turns on the paradox that what is being celebrated can never be experienced again, that its reality is only a memory. Implicit in pastoral is an undying tension between the desire to return to the past and the sober recognition that such a desire can never be fulfilled. Nostalgia is the emotion evinced by pastoral art, and it fuses together the pleasure of remembrance with the painful awareness of mutability. The imaginative tension in *My Ántonia* is perhaps best described as a creative opposition between the novel's content and its form. As the narrator, Jim Burden, tells his life story revolving around the Bohemian immigrant girl, Ántonia Shimerda, he attempts to shape a happy and secure world out of the past by romanticizing disturbing and unpleasant memories. Yet the novel's form, its chronology in five parts, each of which represents a change in time and place in Jim Burden's life, invalidates the narrator's emotional quest, for the passing of time continuously moves the narrator away from the happy point of childhood and brings (for the pastoral imagination) the tragic realization that the past can never be recaptured.

THE TENSION IN CATHER'S PASTORAL VISION

The brief introduction to *My Ántonia*, in which the "author" and the narrator meet on a train traveling across the Midwest, establishes the imaginative tension sustained throughout the novel. As a legal counsel for one of the great western railways Jim Burden frequently has the opportunity of traveling back to the actual scenes of his childhood in Nebraska. In this same vein of retreat we have Willa Cather, the "author," turning over the task of storytelling to a male narrator, thereby effecting in a conventionally acceptable manner a transition to an imaginatively more complete self-identification as a boy. But the introduction also includes a number of details about the narrator's present life which undercut the romantic vision of his childhood and his progress toward success in the world. Here we learn that although Jim spends much of his time traveling across the Midwest, his permanent home is in New York. We also learn that he is married, but his wife is unsympathetic to his quiet tastes and the marriage is sterile and meaningless for him. The brief character sketch of Mrs. Burden as a rich patroness surrounded by a group of mediocre poets and painters prepares us for that moment near the end of the novel when Ántonia, surrounded by her children, asks Jim how many he has. Similarly, the image of Jim restlessly traveling across the country is juxtaposed with the happiness and fixed security of Ántonia's Nebraska farm. Later, as we read Jim's account of his childhood and of his successful progress toward achieving his professional ambitions, we are always aware of the futility of that success in the present. As a temporal framework around the whole novel, the introductory sketch sets up the creative pastoral tension between the memory of past happiness and the experience of loss and estrangement in the present.

THE PASTORAL STRUCTURE

The body of the novel is divided into five parts (books) representing different periods in Jim's life. The pastoral dream of recovering an ideally ordered and timeless world is most closely realized in Book I, in which the narrator describes the first year that he spent on his grandfather's farm in the West and his acquaintance with Ántonia Shimerda. The events and anecdotes that make up this first long section of the novel are imbued with a sense of timelessness and spacelessness, of life once lived beyond the reach of temporal change or the boundaries of a specific place. . . .

Accompanying this sense of spacelessness is a tremendous sense of freedom that is always an integral part of the narrator's descriptions of the landscape. He says that "the road ran about like a wild thing, avoiding the deep draws, crossing them where they were wide and shallow," and reflects that the "sunflower-bordered roads always seem to me the roads to freedom." After killing a rattlesnake and winning Ántonia's praise, he exults in the feeling that "the great land had never looked . . . so big and free." In memory this sense of freedom becomes focused in his relationship with Ántonia, whose wild, impulsive, and generous nature is so much a part of the untamed landscape.

LIVING THROUGH THE SEASONS

More strategic for the recovery of lost childhood is the narrator's elimination of time in this first part. Events and anecdotes are not related to each other in a sequential pattern of cause and effect, but take their direction from the changing seasons. The fact that Book I takes the narrator through one complete cycle of the seasons (Jim arrives in Nebraska in early fall and the section ends the following summer) places his experiences in the context of a cyclical rhythm that is ever-recurring, hence outside of chronological time. Description of landscape in this part continually refers back to a world that has known no historical time: the endless plain covered with tall grass, moving in the wind as if it were a shaggy hide under which galloped herds of wild buffalo, the restless wind in the spring rising and sinking like a playful puppy, the prairie in an autumn sunset like a bush burned with fire but not consumed. Human marks are frail—sod houses and dirt roads; they are of little consequence as measured against the overwhelming landscape. . . .

The romanticizing of time and place is part of an imaginative process at work throughout the novel which either eliminates unpleasant memories or converts them into romantic vignettes. The feeling of "peculiar pleasure" that Pavel's horrific tale gives the narrator is an example. Throughout Book I the harshness of life on the prairie, the very struggle to survive, is softened by Jim's memory as he yearns for a simple mode of existence again. . . .

Book I ends with the dream of all pastorals being voiced. Thinking of her father's death, Ántonia says: "'I wish no winter ever come again.'" And in his optimistic manner Jim reassures her that "it will be summer a long while yet."

Mutability, however, is the *sine qua non* [essential element] of pastoral art, and in the following three parts of the novel the narrator becomes aware of time's passage and feels the restrictions of place. The sense of freedom and romantic horizon disappears from the book: though Jim is growing into manhood and moving out into the world, the world is becoming smaller and setting limitations on him. Book II, "The Hired Girls," takes place three years later when the Burdens have moved into the town of Black Hawk. In the first paragraph describing the town, the narrator refers to his "lost freedom" in leaving the farm. As time passes he feels more and more repressed by the confines of the village and the frustrating mediocrity of its social life. In a despondent mood he reflects on the repression and lack of imagination in the small town. . . .

But the specific conflict that arises for Jim in Book II is

sexual. In pastoral the imagination attempts to exclude sexuality because it is both individual and temporal and leads away from the innocent unified vision of childhood. At first Jim succeeds in his evasion of adult awareness and responsibility. The Burdens live next to the Harlings, a family with five children, and after Ántonia comes to town to work as the Harlings' "hired girl" Jim reflects that he and the other children "were never happier, never felt more contented and secure." The best times for Jim occur when the men are absent—when grandfather is at church and Mr. Harling is away on business—leaving the carefree world of happy chil-

AN ELEGY FOR A LOST ERA

Finding the present to be filled with a sense of emptiness and isolation, Willa Cather re-created a way of life that existed thirty years before she wrote My Ántonia. *For Cather it was a way of life characterized by a noble sense of struggle and endurance, and now irrevocably lost.*

My Ántonia is a novel about the past. James Fenimore Cooper had set *The Deerslayer* a century back in time, Mark Twain had set *Huckleberry Finn* back nearly half a century, and Willa Cather sets the principal part of her novel back some thirty years or more. For all three, whatever their different views of human isolation and their different thematic answers to it, the frontier had disappeared and now belonged to a more heroic time in the past. Willa Cather's past has a particularly nostalgic tint, for it leads to the homesickness of the present. And the nostalgia in turn gives the past a suggestive value, leading, in one sense, to a softness of outline but, in another, to a vividness of impression that makes the moment or the object almost clearer and sharper than life itself. The momentary vision in the novel of the silhouette of a plow against the setting sun, a familiar example of the art of Willa Cather, stands as an example. It is almost too sharp, too perfect, yet it has a high suggestive value that captures the imagination. So, too, the events of Jim Burden's childhood—or Willa Cather's past—stand out in sharp and simplified outline, suggesting a time of heroic dimensions now gone. To this past the novel comes home again from a lonely and isolated present. "Some memories are realities, and are better than anything that can ever happen to one again."

Edwin T. Bowden, *The Dungeon of the Heart: Human Isolation and the American Novel.* New York: MacMillan, 1961, pp. 46–54.

dren presided over by the indulgent Mrs. Harling, the older daughter, Frances, and Ántonia. But Jim is fourteen now, and as narrator he reflects that boys and girls "have to grow up, whether they will or no." The narrator's feelings at this point are again focused in Ántonia; where previously her wild, impulsive nature spelled the unrestricted freedom of childhood, her generous instincts now involve Jim in the complexities of sexuality. A number of the immigrant girls have come to Black Hawk to work as domestics, and to Jim these spontaneous, fun-loving girls (the sensual, slow-moving Lena Lingard, the fast-tripping Tiny Soderball, the three Bohemian Marys of dubious fame) are far more attractive than the repressed and imitative town girls, who have been bred to the social niceties and who seem utterly lacking in vitality. However, the rough manners and irrepressible gaiety of Ántonia and her friends are frowned on by the strict decorum of the town and they are looked upon as distinctly second-class citizens. Jim's potential initiation into sex is thus complicated by social taboo as well as by his preference for remaining a child. The situation comes to a head during "the summer which was to change everything" when the Italian dancing pavilion is set up in Black Hawk. Ántonia loses her place at the Harlings because they disapprove of her dancing and keeping late hours, and she takes a position at the Wick Cutters'. At the same time Jim is forced to sneak off to the Saturday-night dances because of his grandfather's disapproval. There is no doubt that his feeling for the immigrant girls is sexual: he has a recurring erotic dream of Lena in the fields and he kisses Ántonia passionately after one of the Saturday dances. Jim's guilt (in pastoral, sex is always guilt-inducing and destructive) is partly assuaged by Ántonia's playing a motherly and protective role; she warns him against involvement with Lena and encourages him to study diligently at school. But his relationship with the immigrant girls, which becomes a sublimated erotic dalliance during the picnic along the bowery river bank, finally has devastating consequences. Suspicious of her employer's intentions, Ántonia arranges for Jim to sleep in her bed while the Cutters are away. Wick Cutter does in fact return one night to rape Ántonia, but finds himself in a fight with Jim instead. The experience for Jim is disgusting beyond measure; in part it refers him to his own inadmissible desires (one hates most where one sees one's self reflected), but it also taints

Ántonia as a sexual being, and his definition of her as older sister or mother has been spoiled: "I hated her almost as much as I hated Cutter. She had let me in for all this disgustingness." With this sequence Book II abruptly ends.

TRANSLATING THE PAST INTO AN IDEAL

In Book III, "Lena Lingard," Jim is living in Lincoln where he is studying classics at the university. The central emotion of the novel—the increasing sense of loss and alienation as one grows older—is brought to the fore again in the narrator's relationship with the immigrant girls. Significantly, Ántonia, whose image has been sullied by the Cutter affair, does not appear in this part; it is the "forbidden" Lena Lingard, now living in Lincoln as a dressmaker, who visits Jim and revives in him all his feelings about his childhood with Ántonia. But even before Lena appears Jim has begun an imaginative process whereby his past experiences are translated into esthetic forms. As Jim reads the classics with his tutor, Gaston Cleric, his train of thought goes back to his childhood and to the people he had known in the past. He is concerned about these people not for themselves, but as aspects of *his* experience: "They were so much alive in me that I scarcely stopped to wonder whether they were alive anywhere else, or how." The full nature of his concern is revealed when, reading Virgil's *Georgics*, he joins the expression of nostalgia, "the best days are the first to flee," with the artist's statement of purpose, " 'I shall be the first, if I live, to bring the Muse into my country.'" In order to recapture and redeem the past Jim is transforming it into art. The result of the process is, of course, the novel itself—Jim's memoir which he hands over to the "author" in the introduction; but within the narrative there are several instances where an incomplete or disturbing experience becomes an esthetic one. For example, the erotic picnic with the hired girls along the river concludes not in love-making but in the image of the plow against the sun—one of the most powerful images in the novel, which significantly recurs to the narrator as he reads Latin. After Lena's first visit, which quickens his memory of the hired girls, he reflects that "if there were no girls like them in the world, there would be no poetry." Jim's ensuing courtship of Lena takes its signature from art: they attend the theatre together, and one of the plays, *Camille*, which concerns the love of an art student for a woman of the demimonde, reflects something of their own mismatched affair. As another critic has suggested, the whole courtship in Lena's parlor, with the idle talk of fashion, the serving of tea, the nuisance pet dog, the intrusion of older lovers, has the quality of a comedy of manners. But Jim's involvement with Lena becomes more than a diversion—he loses interest in his classes and reading—and rather than risk a distracting and possibly dangerous sexual experience, he follows his tutor to Boston to study at Harvard.

THE LOSS OF INNOCENCE

When Book IV, "The Pioneer Woman's Story," opens, two years have passed and Jim is back in Black Hawk for the summer vacation. In this part he tells us almost nothing of himself except that he will enter Harvard Law School in the fall; but his continuing preoccupation with time and change is reflected in the stories of the immigrant girls, who have been compromised and disillusioned with the passing years. Moving forward for a moment chronologically, the narrator tells us how Lena Lingard and Tiny Soderball both left Black Hawk and achieved material success in the world, but that neither of them were really fulfilled or made happy by it. Tiny made a fortune in the Klondike gold rush and eventually settled in San Francisco, but she never married and had a family. She had numerous exciting adventures in the Klondike, but "the thrill of them was quite gone. She said frankly that nothing interested her much now but making money," and Jim reflects that "she was like someone in whom the faculty of becoming interested is worn out." Lena also does well financially and goes to live near Tiny in San Francisco. Though she has not married either, she is considered a success by the people of Black Hawk because she has profited at dressmaking. These stories remind us of the emptiness of the narrator's own "success."

In contrast to those girls who have spent their lives in pursuit of material security, Ántonia has followed the dictates of her emotions—the result of which is a child born out of wedlock. The narrator, who has not seen her since the time of the Wick Cutter affair, says: "I tried to shut Ántonia out of my mind. I was bitterly disappointed in her." As in the Wick Cutter episode, Ántonia's relationship with the volatile train conductor, Larry Donovan, is sexual, and Jim tries to blot it from his mind. But Ántonia has been abandoned and, after

hearing her pathetic story from the Widow Steavens, Jim decides to visit her before going East again. He finds her working in the fields as he often did when they were children,
and for a place to talk they "instinctively" walk over to the
unplowed patch at the crossroad where Mr. Shimerda is
buried. Jim has forgiven Ántonia, for in his eyes she now re-
sumes her maternal role of older sister and guardian of precious memories from childhood. As they walk homeward
across the field at sunset he wishes he "could be a little boy
again, and that [his] way could end there." After parting
from Antonia and walking on alone, he almost believes "that
a boy and girl ran along beside me, as our shadows used to
do, laughing and whispering to each other in the grass."

RECOVERING PASTORAL TIMELESSNESS

The fifth and last part of the book, "Cuzak's Boys," takes
place twenty years later when Jim, now a railway lawyer, finally stops off in Nebraska for a visit with Ántonia and her
family. At the end of Book IV Jim promised Ántonia that he
would visit her again, but Ántonia was part of his past and
because his memory could fashion out of it a more perfect
order, he avoided a confrontation with its realities. Jim says:
"In the course of twenty crowded years one parts with many
illusions. I did not wish to lose the early ones. Some memories are realities, and are better than anything that can ever
happen to one again." But from the introduction we know
that Jim's life is emotionally empty, so it is not surprising
that when Lena Lingard gives him "a cheerful account of
Ántonia" he decides to risk a visit at last. The implication is
that memory is no longer enough, and that in going back to
Ántonia he is actually trying to relive the past.

In this part the creative tensions in the novel are tautly
balanced: the feeling of transience and alienation effected by
the passing of twenty years runs directly counter to Jim's
pressing urge to eliminate all reminders of time and change.
In Book V the narrator unwittingly attempts nothing less
than to become a boy again and rediscover the happy, timeless world he once knew with Ántonia as his older, protective companion. Here is Willa Cather's intuitive art at its
surest and finest. As Jim nears Ántonia's farm in his buggy
he is greeted by two of Ántonia's boys, reconnecting him to
childhood. They are at the roadside mourning the loss of a
pet dog, but turn their attention at once to the visitor and

lead him up to the farmhouse. Before Ántonia appears Jim looks about and his eye picks up many of the same details he noticed on first awakening in his grandparents' home as a boy: cats sunning themselves, yellow pumpkins on the porch steps, a white kitchen and ducks and geese running across the path (Jim's grandmother moved about quickly as if she were shooing chickens). As in the beginning of the book it is early autumn, the season of fulfillment but also the waning of the year. When Ántonia enters the kitchen, she is not unlike Jim's grandmother in appearance—a stalwart brown woman, spare and aging but vigorous. Jim's stooped grandmother is described as a "woman of unusual endurance," and Ántonia is similarly "battered but not diminished." One of Jim's earliest Nebraska memories is going out to his grandmother's garden a quarter of a mile from the house, and in parallel fashion he is taken almost at once to see the Cuzaks' new cave "a good way from the house," where fruits and vegetables are kept. The past is constantly evoked in the present, for Ántonia has named several of her children after childhood friends, such as Norwegian Anna, Nina Harling, her sister Yulka, and her brother Ambrosch.

ELIMINATING SEXUALITY

Jim's persistent idealization of Ántonia as a mother figure is fully and legitimately realized now. Surrounded by her children who come running out of the fruit cave like "a veritable explosion of life," Ántonia's maternal nature assumes almost mythic dimension. Standing in the orchard with her hand on one of the trees she has carefully nurtured, she suggests both earth-mother and fertility goddess. Jim reflects "that she was a rich mine of life, like the founders of early races." On the other hand, he feels more than ever like a boy again and Ántonia says to him appropriately: " 'You've kept so young.'" He in turn delights in Ántonia's young sons and chooses to sleep with them in the haymow rather than in the house. He says: "I felt like a boy in their company, and all manner of forgotten interests revived in me." He takes most interest in the mischievous Leo, who, like Jim, is intensely jealous of Ántonia's affection and whom Ántonia confesses she likes the best. In accord with Jim's deepest wishes Ántonia's husband is conveniently away the first day, and sitting under the grape arbor in Ántonia's orchard with its triple enclosure of wire, locust, and mulberry hedges, Jim finds a perfect pastoral haven and "deepest peace." Ántonia's husband, however, does not disrupt the harmony of Jim's visit, for he poses no masculine threat. He is described as a "crumpled little man" without much force, and Jim soon calls him "Papa" with the rest. In Cuzak's relation to Ántonia there is no suggestion of sex: theirs is a friendship in which he is simply "the instrument of Ántonia's special mission" of procreation. The elimination of sexuality is thoroughgoing. The one sexual incident in Jim's life relating to Ántonia is rendered comic when one of the children tells Jim about the grotesque end to Wick Cutter's life. In similar comic fashion Jim is told that Ántonia's aggressive brother Ambrosch has been unmanned by a fat, rich wife who bosses him about.

When Jim leaves Ántonia's farm and goes back to Black Hawk his mood is temporarily broken: he finds so many things changed—friends dead or moved away, old trees cut down, strange children in the Harling yard—that he is confronted again with the fact of time's passage. But he does not remain in town for long; he goes out into the country to a place where the landscape has remained unchanged and where his romantic, esthetic eye can transform it once again into the thing of beauty and permanence that his imagination craves. . . .

CHILDHOOD REGAINED

In Ántonia's family he has found a connection with his own childhood again: "There were enough Cuzaks to play with for a long while yet. Even after the boys grew up, there would always be Cuzak himself!" As he looks at the old road he first traveled with Ántonia he philosophically complements his feelings of having come home again by envisioning life as a circle which invariably returns a man to his beginnings. The novel is a pastoral of innocence for it asserts that life's greatest values are to be found in childhood. Our response to this final emotion is ambiguous, and therein lies the greatness of the novel. Aware of the impossibility of returning to childhood and recovering innocence, we are nonetheless drawn, like Jim Burden, to Ántonia and her farm; but unlike Jim we can never quite evade the poignant realization that we have already gone beyond, and that Ántonia and her family lie in the precious but irrecoverable past.

An American Epic

John H. Randall III

Cather's Nebraska novels, highlighting as they do the richness of a geographical location previously over-looked in American literature, are in many ways a continuation of the American regionalist movement. In this excerpt, John H. Randall III illustrates the extent to which Cather also wants to infuse the lives of her characters with a universal significance. She does so by invoking such legendary figures as the Spanish explorer Coronado and Virgil, the first great poet of ancient Rome. In the course of the novel, Jim comes to realize that the achievements of the Nebraska settlers, of which the "hired girls" are such an essential component, are great unsung events in the history of America, if not the world. John H. Randall III was a professor of English at Boston University. His book *The Landscape and the Looking Glass: Willa Cather's Search for Value* (1960) was influential in reviving interest in Cather's contribution to American literature.

The gay country girls come to signify for [Jim Burden] the joyful expansiveness of country life as opposed to the contraction of the circle of living which oppresses him so much in town. The highest point of the book's middle section occurs when he goes with Ántonia and the hired girls on a picnic. They spend an idyllic day by the shores of the river, and in a long passage meant to celebrate the joys of country living the girls point out their fathers' farms to him, talk about them, and boast of the things they are going to get for their families. Then comes the passage which is meant to be the climax:

> "Jim," Ántonia said dreamily, "I want you to tell the girls about how the Spanish first came here, like you and Charley Harling used to talk about. I've tried to tell them, but I leave out so much."

They sat under a little oak, Tony resting against the trunk and the other girls leaning against her and each other, and listened to the little I was able to tell them about Coronado and his search for the Seven Golden Cities. At school we were taught that he had given up his quest and turned back somewhere in Kansas. But Charley Harling and I had a strong belief that he had been along this very river. A farmer in the county north of ours, when he was breaking sod, had turned up a metal stirrup of fine workmanship, and a sword with a Spanish inscription on the blade. He lent these relics to Mr. Harling, who brought them home with him. Charley and I scoured them, and they were on exhibition in the Harling office all summer. Father Kelly, the priest, had found the name of the Spanish maker on the sword, and an abbreviation that stood for the city of Cordova.

"And that I saw with my own eyes," Ántonia put in triumphantly. "So Jim and Charley were right, and the teachers were wrong!"

The girls began to wonder among themselves. Why had the Spaniards come so far? What must this country have been like, then? Why had Coronado never gone back to Spain, to his riches and his castles and his king? I couldn't tell them. I only knew the school books said he "died in the wilderness, of a broken heart."

"More than him has done that," said Ántonia sadly, and the girls murmured assent.

We sat looking off across the country, watching the sun go down. The curly grass about us was on fire now. The bark of the oaks turned red as copper. There was a shimmer of gold on the brown river. Out in the stream the sandbars glittered like glass, and the light trembled in the willow thickets as if little flames were leaping among them. The breeze sank to stillness. In the ravine a ringdove mourned plaintively, and somewhere off in the bushes an owl hooted. The girls sat listless, leaning against each other. The long fingers of the sun touched their foreheads.

Presently we saw a curious thing: There were no clouds, and the sun was going down in a limpid, gold-washed sky. Just as the lower edge of the red disc rested on the high fields against the horizon, a great black figure suddenly appeared on the face of the sun. We sprang to our feet, straining our eyes toward it. In a moment we realized what it was. On some upland farm, a plough had been left standing in the field. The sun was sinking just behind it. Magnified across the distance by the horizontal light, it stood out against the sun, was exactly contained within the circle of the disc; the handles, the tongue, the share—black against the molten red. There it was, heroic in size, a picture writing on the sun.

Even while we whispered about it, our vision disappeared; the ball dropped and dropped until the red tip went beneath

the earth. The fields below us were forgotten, the sky was
growing pale, and that forgotten plough had sunk back to its
own littleness somewhere on the prairie.

THE PLOUGH AGAINST THE SUN

Coronado stands for the spirit of adventure and romance,
and the kind of life young people dream about. The pedantic
mind, which is the enemy of Coronado and all his kind, de-
nied that that Spanish *conquistador* had ever set foot between the Republican River and the river Platte; Nebraska, it
holds, is too mundane ever to have been part of the realms
of romance. But the young people's own experience gives
this the lie; they are sure Coronado has been along this very
river, and sure enough, a Spanish sword is plowed up, with
an inscription and an abbreviation of Cordova on the blade.
So the spirit of romance has been to this dry, flat country;
but the spirit of romance is not enough. It can see things, but
it cannot persevere. Coronado never did find what he was
looking for, but died in the wilderness of a broken heart. But
if the spirit of romance had been to this country, so has the
spirit of civilization. This is symbolized by the plough
against the sun. The agricultural implement is made the
symbol of a whole way of life; as it stands with its tongue
and shares contained within the circle of the sun it becomes
representative of everything Willa Cather has been glorify-
ing. Willa Cather prepares for this symbol, as she does for
others, by the use of light as a transfiguring agent. The world
as seen under ordinary light, the common light of day, looks
as ordinary and commonplace as the pedantic mind can
conceive of it as being, but when illuminated by some special kind of light, such as sunset, it becomes transfigured
and the real glory that lies latent in everyday things is
brought out. In this manner a perfectly ordinary, homely
farming tool is made the symbol of a settled agricultural civilization, which is thereby given a kind of cosmic approval.

Coronado and the plough against the sun are two oppo-
sites which, taken together, are meant to embrace the whole
of life; neither one is sufficient alone, but together they suf-
fice. Coronado had his heart broken by the plains country,
but the plough conquered it. In her choice of the plough as a
symbol, Willa Cather shows that the people she is most interested in are not the nomadic pioneers but the tillers of the
soil who come after them; her symbol stands in marked

contrast to the hunting dog and musket grouped around the dying Leatherstocking at the end of [James Fenimore] Cooper's novel, *The Prairie*.

VIRGIL AND NEBRASKA

Jim Burden now fully realizes the superiority of country life to life in a small town, but so far he has little acquaintance with the world outside the rural areas: his vision is still bounded by the horizon of his neighbors' cornfields. Desperately wanting to get into the great world outside, he looks forward to going off to Lincoln to attend the university. Once there, he finds out what an important part the countryside has played in the history of civilization itself. He falls under the influence of Gaston Cleric, a brilliant young scholar newly made head of the Latin department. Cleric introduces him to the great artistic tradition of the Western world, the tradition of ornate dignity and the grand style stemming ultimately from Virgil. It is from him that Jim learns that the word "patria" has a purely local meaning, and that Virgil had loved the little rural neighborhood as much as he himself loved his grandparents' farm. He begins to get some faint glimmering of the way in which human existence is the same in all times and at all places, but he does not yet know how to correlate art and life.

> Although I admired scholarship so much in Cleric, I was not deceived about myself; I knew that I should never be a scholar. I never could lose myself for long among impersonal things. Mental excitement was apt to send me with a rush back to my own naked land and the figures scattered upon it. While I was in the very act of yearning toward the new forms that Cleric brought up before me, my mind plunged away from me, and I suddenly found myself thinking of the places and people of my own infinitesimal past. They stood out, strengthened and simplified now, like the image of the plough against the sun. They were all I had for an answer to the new appeal. I begrudged the room that Jake and Otto and Russian Peter took up in my memory, which I wanted to crowd with other things. But whenever my consciousness was quickened, all those early friends were quickened within it, and in some strange way they accompanied me through all my new experiences. They were so much alive in me that I scarcely stopped to wonder whether they were alive anywhere else, or how.

. . . Jim Burden considers the things he knows about to be supremely unimportant, and the things he doesn't know about to be of crucial importance. He underrates his own past and is irate when the people in it keep bobbing up in his consciousness. What do Otto Fuchs and Russian Peter have to do with Virgil? It is too early for him to know that his little world is part of the great world; he hasn't yet seen that his life is not unique but that he is part of humanity. He still doesn't understand his background, but he is beginning to realize that it is important.

VIRGIL'S POETRY AND THE "HIRED GIRLS"

In his second year at Lincoln, Jim has an experience which helps to clarify for him the relation between life and art. Lena Lingard, one of the country girls he admires so much, comes to Lincoln and they strike up a friendship. On the evening of her first visit he is already in the mood to see new relations between things:

> One March evening in my Sophomore year I was sitting alone in my room after supper. . . . On the edge of the prairie, where the sun had gone down, the sky was turquoise blue, like a lake, with gold light throbbing in it. Higher up, in the utter clarity of the western slope, the evening star hung like a lamp suspended by silver chains—like the lamp engraved upon the title page of old Latin texts, which is always appearing in new heavens, and awakening new desires in men.

By the very act of thinking of such a comparison, he is beginning to see how his life fits in with the classic past.

> I propped my book open and stared listlessly at the page of the Georgics where tomorrow's lesson began. It opened with the melancholy reflection that, in the lives of mortals, the best days are the first to flee. "Optima dies . . . prima fugit."

Then Lena Lingard knocks at the door, and for a time Jim is dragged back very pleasantly into the present. He has had recurrent dreams about Lena, and now the dreams seem about to translate themselves into reality. He and she have some kind of love experience together, but Willa Cather gingerly avoids telling us of what it consists. After Lena leaves, he realizes for the first time that the things he has experienced are the kind of things people write about, that literature is a reflection of the experience of real people, and that life and art coincide:

> When I turned back to my room the place seemed much pleasanter than before. Lena had left something warm and friendly in the lamplight. How I loved to hear her laugh again! . . . When I closed my eyes I could hear them all laughing—the Danish laundry girls and the three Bohemian

Marys. Lena had brought them all back to me. It came over me, as it had never done before, the relation between girls like those and the poetry of Virgil. If there were no girls like them in the world, there would be no poetry. I understood that clearly, for the first time.

Jim Burden has a great insight as he stands in his room after Lena has gone. In seeing the relation between girls like her and Virgil's *Georgics* he has made a discovery important enough to rank as a creative act: he has succeeded in bringing Nebraska in line with the great tradition. And the great tradition—as Willa Cather sees it, at least—is a rural tradition; one need only think of the importance which the Virgil of the *Georgics* and the Horace of the *Odes* gave to the countryside. No longer does Jim have to feel like a young man from the provinces who comes up to the metropolis and is looked down upon, nor does he have to accept the inferiority of America to Europe; he has seen the unity of all life and all art everywhere; he has seen the ultimate unity of human experience.

THE GARDEN OF THE WORLD

If one of the main themes of *My Ántonia* is the superiority of the countryside and the excellence of rural life, the chief image that Willa Cather uses to express that excellence is one we have already come across in discussing *O Pioneers!:* that of the garden of the world. It is in fact the basic metaphor of the whole book; everything in the novel leads up to the final section in which Ántonia has become the mistress of a large and fertile farm.

The garden image is present in the minds of both Willa Cather and some of her characters. Not the least of Grandfather Burden's insights is his ability to understand the larger meaning of the enterprise in which he and his neighbors are engaged. To the hundreds of thousands of toiling individuals who settled the West it must have seemed that each of them was seeking solely to improve his own lot, but according to the thinking of the time they were actually fulfilling a much larger destiny. The settlement of America was considered to be a part of a divine plan. When the great basin of the Mississippi Valley was completely populated, it was to become not only an earthly paradise for the inhabitants, who would thus live in a latter-day Garden of Eden, but also the whole earth's granary; by means of its immense fertility it would feed the people of Europe and Asia as well. Willa Cather had hinted at this in *O Pioneers!;* in *My Ántonia* she makes it quite explicit:

> July came on with the breathless, brilliant heat which makes the plains of Kansas and Nebraska the best corn country in the world. It seemed as if we could hear the corn growing in the night; under the stars one caught a faint crackling in the dewy, heavy-odored cornfields where the feathered stalks stood so juicy and green. If all the great plain from the Missouri to the Rocky Mountains had been under glass, and the heat regulated by a thermometer, it could not have been better for the yellow tassels that were ripening and fertilizing each other day by day. The cornfields were far apart in those times, with miles of wild grazing land between. It took a clear, meditative eye like my grandfather's to foresee that they would enlarge and multiply until they would be, not the Shimerdas' cornfields, or Mr. Bushy's but the world's cornfields; that their yield would be one of the great economic facts, like the wheat crop of Russia, which underlie all the activities of men, in peace or war.

This is one way in which Willa Cather adjusts Nebraska to the macrocosm and gives local happenings a cosmic importance.

The Inset Stories and the Presence of Evil

Michael Peterman

The "stories within the story" of *My Ántonia* are powerful, memorable, and characterized by shocking violence. The major question that arises is why the gruesome tale of Peter and Pavel and Ántonia's recounting of a tramp who throws himself into a threshing machine are there at all; for all their effectiveness, they do seem strangely detached from the novel. Michael Peterman argues that the inset stories serve a psychological function. Representing real-life episodes in the form of oral narrative both engages listeners and distances them from unpleasantness by giving them a safe role as an audience. By listening to and telling these stories, Jim and Ántonia are initiated into the violent and often evil dimensions of human life, and therefore the stories contribute to their growth and maturity. Michael Peterman teaches English at Trent University, and has published work on Robertson Davies and Catherine Parr Traill.

In particular, the story of Peter and Pavel galvanizes attention. "What does it mean?" "Why is it there?" "How does it relate to the novel as a whole?" So haunting and powerful is the wolf story that, as [critic] Susan Rosowski has recently observed, "it is often the single episode people remember years after first reading *My Ántonia*.". . .

How "random" are these vignettes? One should, of course, acknowledge Cather's own wryly self-conscious remark, "If you gave me a thousand dollars for every structural flaw in *My Ántonia* you'd make me very rich." At the same time one can direct students to the careful and challenging interpretations of recent critics like David Stouck and Blanche

Excerpted from Michael Peterman, "Kindling the Imagination: The Inset Stories of *My Ántonia*," in *Approaches to Teaching Cather's* My Ántonia, edited by Susan Rosowski. Reprinted with permission from the Modern Language Association of America.

Gelfant, both of whom see imaginative patterns at work in the vignettes. Focusing particularly on Cather's use of certain of these episodes or inset stories in the novel's first two sections, this essay sees such experiences as implicit steps, or building blocks, in the shaping not only of the individual imaginations of Jim and Ántonia but also of the special relationship between them on which later, often disturbing events crucially depend.

THE INSET STORIES ARE SHARED EXPERIENCES

In directing specific attention to these inset stories, I begin by calling attention to the description of the cedar tree that Jake brings home for Jim's first Nebraska Christmas. Decorated in the unexpected splendors from Otto's cowboy trunk, "Our tree," as Jim recalls, "became the talking tree of the fairy tale; legends and stories nestled like birds in its branches." The image is, I suggest, a clue to what Cather aims to make of the early stages of her narrative—the book is to be the talking tree of the shared immigrant experience of Ántonia and Jim. It is explicitly a story about the "freemasonry" of youth, designed to encompass vividly and suggestively "the country, the conditions, the whole *adventure* of *our* childhood" (emphases added). "Freemasonry," the crucial word in the introduction, establishes the emphasis on instinctive sympathies and fellowship, on those shared adventures, be they experiences undergone or stories heard, that draw Ántonia and Jim ever closer together emotionally and imaginatively.

For both Jim and Ántonia, Nebraska offers so violent a change from past experience that, though they are ten and fourteen respectively when they arrive, their adventures come to them freshly, with the force of first things. Nebraska is their Robinson Crusoe's island, their Swiss family Robinson's jungle. While Ántonia's disjunction is cultural and linguistic, Jim's is severe enough that, faced by a landscape very different from Virginia, he feels that "I had left even [the] spirits [of my dead parents] behind me." As new friends in "a new world," they share experiences and adventures with an openness, freshness, and passion that is at once believable and deeply affecting. By age as well as by the Old World distinction represented by her father, Ántonia has an advantage that sufficiently distances her from Jim in sexual matters, rendering her more like an older, watchful, and sensitive sister. Moreover, she is his entrée into the realities of immigrant experience. By circumstance, Jim is initially her teacher of English and her guide to the confusing labyrinth of American ways. Each has much to offer the other. As their lives unfold and develop, this continues to be true. The beauty the novel celebrates is the relationship they create and, against the march of time, sustain.

THE PSYCHOLOGICAL DIMENSION OF "STORIES"

From the cedar tree, I find it useful to move to [psychologist] Bruno Bettelheim. In *The Uses of Enchantment*, Bettelheim argues that the sustaining sense of "meaning in our lives," what constitutes "a secure understanding of what the meaning of one's life may or ought to be," is the product of a long development: psychological maturity, like wisdom, "is built up, small step by small step, from most irrational beginnings." Though in *My Ántonia* Cather is not precisely concerned with either children or fairy tales—the absence of the healthful experience of unsugared fairy tales in the experience of most modern children is Bettelheim's major concern—she brings to her presentation of Jim and Ántonia's Nebraska experience a sensitivity to the process of psychological development that Bettelheim is helpful in explicating. Fairy tales and mythical stories have throughout human history constituted much of a child's intellectual life. Avoiding overt didacticism, such stories "relate to all aspects of the child's personality," presenting human problems in so simplified and typical a manner that they give full credence to the seriousness of children's predicaments and allow them the opportunity to begin to understand themselves, to create a sense of order sufficient to sustain them in life. The implicit message of fairy tales is one that the child discovers independently:

> that a struggle against severe difficulties in life is unavoidable, is an intrinsic part of human existence—but that if one does not shy away, but steadfastly meets unexpected and often unjust hardships, one masters all obstacles and at the end emerges victorious.

In her depiction of the episodes that define the relationship between Ántonia and Jim, Cather anticipates Bettelheim while avoiding his solemnity. She recognizes that certain stories or experiences can facilitate the growth of personal identity, especially if they are assimilated as experience. As Bettelheim notes,

Explaining to a child why a fairy tale is so captivating to him destroys ... the story's enchantment, which depends to a considerable degree on the child's not quite knowing why he is delighted by it. And with the forfeiture of this power to enchant goes also a loss of the story's potential for helping the child struggle on his own, and master all by himself the problem which has made the story meaningful to him in the first place.

PAVEL, PETER, AND THE WOLVES

The Peter-Pavel episode provides a striking case in point. Cather implicitly establishes its importance by giving it early prominence in the narrative. Also implicitly, she suggests that such a story, while not formally a fairy tale, has a tremendous emotional and imaginative power for both Jim and Ántonia. The immediacy of suffering and death and the horrific details deeply fascinate them. Later in the novel Cather is careful to remind us of this capacity in young people to entertain the gruesome when Ántonia's children greet a retelling of the Cutter murder-suicide with cheers of "Hurrah! The murder!" More significant still, the Peter-Pavel story has a special place in the "freemasonry" of Ántonia and Jim's relationship. As Jim recounts, "we talked of nothing else for days afterward" except "our Pavel and Peter." Later he adds,

> For Ántonia and me, the story of the wedding party was never at an end. We did not tell Pavel's secret to anyone, but guarded it jealously—as if the wolves of the Ukraine had gathered that night long ago, and the wedding party been sacrificed, to give us a painful and peculiar pleasure.

It is a measure of Cather's fine judgment, her artistic tact, that she nowhere tries to interpret what, if anything, Pavel's story might mean. We know that Pavel is delirious when he tells it to Mr. Shimerda. Realistically, we might well question the story's assertions in that it would be a rare pack of wolves that would run down seven sledges one by one. But as preposterous as the events appear to be, the story is the more powerful—and must have seemed so to Cather—because of its "awful" elements and because of the conditions in which it is heard. The death-bed raging and confession, the despair of dying so far from home, the sense of innocence betrayed, the ferocious urge to survive, the awe of entering into dark and forbidden secrets all contribute to the effect on the young people. . . .

At the same time, to the impressionable Jim, Peter and Pavel seem to be dogged by a relentless destiny. "Misfortune," he notes, "seemed to settle like an evil bird on the roof of the log house, and to flap its wings there, warning human beings away." Theirs is above all a story of immigrant defeat. It is especially telling on Ántonia's father, whose misfortune it is to bear the full weight of middle-aged exile and whose gruesome suicide is anticipated by the Russians' conspicuous failure.

For Ántonia and Jim, by contrast, the story becomes something quite different. It is a part of their mutual treasure hoard. Without this shared and haunting episode we would have far less sense of why Jim feels so strong a kinship with Ántonia. Few of their experiences would seem to have united them more. And, if we accept Bettelheim's notion that young people learn in their own ways through undidactic tales, we might well argue that the lesson implicit in the tale is to avoid jettisoning the bride and groom, to avoid, in short, betrayal of one's closest friends. Jim's concluding remarks about the vignette subtly suggest the way in which the story has taken a special hold on his particular landscape: "At night, before I went to sleep, I often found myself in a sledge drawn by three horses, dashing through a country that looked something like Nebraska and something like Virginia."

ÁNTONIA'S TALE OF THE TRAMP

Another vignette of similar gruesomeness is Ántonia's account of the tramp's suicide in the threshing machine. It belongs in the narrative to Ántonia's days in Black Hawk with the Harlings and gives a special warm flavor to Cather's presentation of life in that home. Through its telling Ántonia emerges still more clearly in her role as powerful storyteller, as agent of the oral tradition Cather carefully integrates into the freemasonry of an early Nebraska upbringing. We remember that it was Ántonia who translated and told Pavel's story to Jim, who recounts Jim's killing of the rattlesnake (another episode worth attention) "with a great deal of colour," and who, through her "stories and entertainment," later inspires a similar kind of excitement in her children. She tells her stories engagingly and innocently, as if somehow, however great their intrinsic fascination, they cannot be explained. (The same qualities are apparent in Rudolph's telling of the Cutter murder.) For Jim, "Everything she said seemed to come right out of her heart."

In looking closely at the details of the tramp story, one is again struck by Cather's care in her placement of the episode as well as by the restraint of her presentation. Pavel's story is told in late autumn with winter approaching, anticipatory of Mr. Shimerda's suicide. Though its event occurs in the heat of harvest, the tramp story is a winter's tale that anticipates the different kind of madness to be found in Wick Cutter.

The tramp comes upon the threshing at Ole Iverson's. Seeing him first, Ántonia senses from his eyes, which were "awful red and wild, like he had some sickness," and his sardonic remarks, that he is "crazy." Ignoring her warnings, Ole allows the tramp up on the thresher, whereupon, after cutting a few bands, "he waved his hand to me and jumped head-first right into the threshing machine after the wheat." What fascinates about the story is at once its power to shock, its economic use of detail, and its innocent mode of telling. Ántonia recounts her adventure directly to Mrs. Harling, effectively dramatizing the "basic harmony" between hired girl and mistress, and the special place Ántonia has won in her home. The few details—the tramp's expression of disgust with immigrants in "Americy," his wave, the fact that the machine never worked right thereafter, and the contents of his pockets—provide apparent clues to his action but allow for no coherent explanation. Why, we wonder, did his possessions include only an old penknife, a wishbone, and a worn copy of "The Old Oaken Bucket"? . . . What happens, we wonder, to the poem that is, in the story's aftermath, the one detail that transfixes the listeners?

The power of the tramp story lies as much in its gruesomeness, which causes Nina Harling to cry, as in its mysteriousness. Innocently Ántonia herself voices the question, "Now, wasn't that strange . . . ? What would anybody want to kill themselves in summer for? In threshing time, too! It's nice everywhere then." There is no available answer. Alcoholism, failure, despair, and alienation suggest themselves, but only partially. Ántonia's response, which implies Jim's as well, is a healthy one. The experience, transmuted into a story, has, if anything, deepened her commitment to life. Much as Bettelheim suggests in *The Uses of Enchantment,* disquieting realities serve to develop or reinforce positive, healthful ideas and beliefs.

THE INSET STORIES CONTRIBUTE
TO JIM AND ÁNTONIA'S GROWTH

The episodes that play a prominent part in the early sections of *My Ántonia* are not mere inset stories or fascinating digressions. They are delicately placed steps or building blocks that image and characterize the rich and enduring relationship between Ántonia and Jim. They provide a sense of that special cohesiveness, so much so that these memories live as freshly for Jim in the present as they originally did. In such episodes, so often related to story telling, Cather captures not only the felt appeal of adventures shared but the instinctive sympathy between Jim and Ántonia that is near the novel's center. And while such episodes give amplitude to the pastoral paradox that David Stouck develops in detail, Cather's control is such, I would argue, that she does not "romanticiz[e] disturbing and unpleasant memories." Rather, she allows the reader to infer from their presentation the healthful ways in which Ántonia and Jim imaginatively transmute such experiences. The novel offers stages in growth, not instances of evasion.

"Art is a concrete and personal and childish thing after all," Cather wrote in her unfinished essay "Light on Adobe Walls." Those properties are evident in the narrative steps by which she unobtrusively and evocatively takes us into the feel of events and stories—things done and things heard—that together engender the extraordinary sense of friendship and kinship at the heart of *My Ántonia.*

The Struggle to Maintain Innocence

Robert E. Scholes

Innocence, self-knowledge as loss of innocence, and an attachment to the idea of beginning anew in an unknown environment are themes that are repeated countless times in American literature. In the following essay, Robert E. Scholes illustrates the extent to which the innocence of Jim, Ántonia, and the "hired girls" evolves into a sense of nostalgia for times past, as the struggles of the original pioneers in a harsh new land begin to bear fruit. Something intangible has been lost as the next generation, no longer required to undertake the sacrifices of the first, lacks the resolve and heroism of the original founders of Black Hawk. Yet Scholes maintains that Ántonia manages to elude this nostalgia for innocence lost and thrive in the present. In contrast, the materially successful Jim, Lena, and Tiny are more ambivalent about the past. Robert E. Scholes is a professor of English at Brown University. He has written and edited more than thirty books, from studies of James Joyce and Ernest Hemingway to highly influential works on structuralist theories of literature.

The American Innocent was a major preoccupation of American novelists from James and Howells down to Willa Cather and F. Scott Fitzgerald. And it may be useful to examine exactly how one novelist, Willa Cather, made use of the Adamic myth in her fullest treatment of it: *My Antonia.*

As [critic R.W.B.] Lewis distills it, the myth of Adam in America is that of an "individual emancipated from history, happily bereft of ancestry, untouched and undefiled by the usual inheritances of family and race; an individual standing alone, self-propelling, ready to confront whatever

Excerpted from Robert E. Scholes, "Hope and Memory in *My Ántonia*," *Shenandoah*, vol. 14, no. 1, 1962. Reprinted from *Shenandoah:* The Washington and Lee University Review, with permission of the Editor.

awaited him with the aid of his own unique and inherent resources." This Adamic person is "thrust into an actual world and an actual age," and, in the fully developed myth, undergoes a "fall": suffers "the necessary transforming shocks and sufferings, the experiments and errors . . . through which maturity and identity may be arrived at." Mr. Lewis is a bit mysterious about what he means by "identity," but self-knowledge or self-discovery are probably safe, if not totally accurate, substitutes.

JIM AND ANTONIA AS INNOCENTS

The two central figures in *My Antonia* are, in different senses, Innocents. Jim Burden, bereft of both his parents within a year, is removed from the warm and comfortable Virginia of his early days and thrust into the strange and frightening world of Nebraska. As he bumps along on the wagon ride to his new home, he feels that he has left even the spirits of his dead parents behind him:

> The wagon jolted on, carrying me I know not whither. I don't think I was homesick. If we never arrived anywhere, it did not matter. Between that earth and that sky I felt erased, blotted out. I did not say my prayers that night: here, I felt, what would be would be.

Antonia Shimerda, though also a young, innocent creature in a raw country, is not bereft of the past as Jim Burden is. Antonia's Bohemian ancestry is a part of her and exerts a decided influence on her present and future. We are reminded of this past constantly: by the Bohemian customs and culinary practices of the Shimerdas; by the observations of Otto Fuchs on the relationship of Austrians and Bohemians in the old country; and especially by the Catholic religion of the Bohemians, which is their strongest link with the past, and which serves to bind them together and to separate them from the Protestant society of their adopted land. But, most important, Antonia herself cherishes her connection with the past. When Jim asks if she remembers the little town of her birth, she replies,

> "Jim . . . if I was put down there in the middle of the night, I could find my way all over that little town; and along the river where my grandmother lived. My feet remember all the little paths through the woods, and where the big roots stick out to trip you. I ain't never forgot my own country."

But despite the importance of the past for Antonia, she and the other hired girls are figures of heroic and vital innocence, associated with nature and the soil. Like Lena Lingard, they all "waked fresh with the world every day." They are unused to the ways of society, and Antonia, especially, is too trusting. Lena tells Jim that Antonia "won't hear a word against [Larry Donovan]. She's so sort of innocent." The struggle of the "hired girls" with society is one of the important themes of the novel. Jim Burden remarks that

> the country girls were considered a menace to the social order. Their beauty shone out too boldly against a conventional background. But anxious mothers need have felt no alarm. They mistook the mettle of their sons. The respect for respectability was stronger than any desire in Black Hawk youth.

THE HIRED GIRLS, THE CITY, AND THE LAND

This struggle of the country girls with the city is a very perplexing one, in which apparent victory and apparent defeat are both apt to prove evanescent in time. Lena Lingard and Tiny Soderball become successful, triumphing even in the metropolis of San Francisco, while Antonia becomes the foolish victim of her love for a conniving railroad conductor. But Lena and Tiny succeed only in becoming more like the society from which they had been ostracized, while Antonia, and the other country girls who stay on the land, ultimately change the structure of society itself. Jim Burden remarks,

> I always knew I should live long enough to see my country girls come into their own, and I have. Today the best that a harassed Black Hawk merchant can hope for is to sell provisions and farm machinery and automobiles to the rich farms where that first crop of stalwart Bohemian and Scandinavian girls are now the mistresses.

Jim Burden, like Lena and Tiny, has made his success in the city and on the city's terms. From the narrator of the introductory chapter we learn that Jim's personal life, his marriage, has not been a success though his legal work flourishes. Jim's failure to find happiness or satisfaction in his career and in the city, constitutes for him the "fall" into self-knowledge which is characteristic of the Adamic hero. It is Jim's recognition of his own fall that makes him superior to Lena and Tiny, and enables him to live vicariously through Antonia and her children.

Antonia's seduction is a more clear-cut "fall" than Jim's unhappiness, and her subsequent self-knowledge is more strikingly evidenced. When Jim meets Antonia after she has had her illegitimate child, he notices "a new kind of strength in the gravity of her face." At this meeting she asks Jim whether he has learned to like big cities, adding that she would die of lonesomeness in such a place. "I like to be where I know every stack and tree, and where all the ground is friendly," she says; and after they part Jim feels "the old pull of the earth, the solemn magic that comes out of those fields at night-fall," and he wishes he could be a little boy again, and that his way would end there.

A RETURN TO THE PAST

When Jim revisits Antonia and her thriving family, she has in some ways relapsed toward the past. "'I've forgot my English so.'" She says, "'I don't often talk it any more. I tell the children I used to speak it real well.' She said they all spoke Bohemian at home. The little ones could not speak English at all—didn't learn it until they went to school." But her children, her involvement in life, makes her concerned for the future. She has lived "much and hard," reflects Jim as they meet, but "she was there, in the full vigor of her personality, battered but not diminished, looking at me, speaking to me in the husky, breathy voice I remembered so well." Jim, however, is not recognized by Antonia at first, even though he has "kept so young." He is less battered, perhaps, but he is more diminished.

So it is that Antonia, who is always conscious of the past, is nevertheless free of it, and capable of concern for the future. And her past is not merely that of a generation or so. Jim observes, "She lent herself to immemorial human attitudes which we recognize by instinct as universal and true. . . . It was no wonder that her sons stood tall and straight. She was a rich mine of life, like the founders of early races." Whereas Jim, who has no such connection with the past, who came to Nebraska without a family and rode on a wagon into a new life which he felt was beyond even the attention of God, is still bound by the recent past, by what has happened to him in his own youth, and he lives in both the present and the future only vicariously through the plans and lives of others. He reflects, "In the course of twenty crowded years one parts with many illusions. I did not wish to lose the early ones. Some memories are realities, and are better than anything that can happen to one again." Jim is haunted by the past, by the sense that, in the phrase of Virgil which is the novel's epigraph, *Optima dies . . . prima fugit.* When he contemplates in the closing lines of his narrative the road on which he had entered his new life as a boy, he reconsiders his whole existence:

I had the sense of coming home to myself, and of having found out what a little circle man's experience is. For Antonia and for me, this had been the road of Destiny; had taken us to those early accidents of fortune which predetermined for us all that we can ever be. Now I understood that the same road was to bring us together again. Whatever we had missed, we possessed together the precious, the incommunicable past.

THE SADNESS OF NOSTALGIA

Antonia's life is not tragic. She is neither defeated nor destroyed by life, not even diminished. Yet the distinguishing characteristic of this novel is its elegiac tone; the eternal note of sadness pervades especially the closing passages of the book. The direct cause of this element of sadness is the nostalgia of Jim Burden, through which the story of Antonia filters down to the reader. But behind Jim Burden's nostalgia, and merged with it, is the nostalgia of Willa Cather herself.

There is a suggestion in this novel and in the earlier *O Pioneers!* that the younger brothers and the sisters of this splendid generation of pioneer women will not be their equals. Emil Bergson—the youth in *O Pioneers!* for whom his older sister Alexandra labors and plans—attends the university, escapes from the plough, only to ruin several lives through his adulterous love. And in *My Antonia* there is the suggestion that the coming generations will be less heroic and more ordinary than the present breed. Jim Burden at one point muses on this problem, thinking of the hired girls in Black Hawk:

> Those girls had grown up in the first bitter-hard times, and had got little schooling themselves. But the younger brothers and sisters, for whom they made such sacrifices and who have had "advantages," never seem to me, when I meet them now, half as interesting or as well educated. The older girls, who helped to break up the wild sod, learned so much from life, from poverty, from their mothers and grandmothers; they had all, like Antonia, been early awakened and made observant by coming at a tender age from an old country to a new.

The circumstances which formed Antonia will not be repeated; the future will be in the hands of a diminished race. It is the feeling which haunts Willa Cather's novel. Antonia looks to the future of her children, but Jim Burden knows that the future will be at best a poor imitation of the past. Antonia's life is a triumph of innocence and vitality over hardship and evil. But Willa Cather does not celebrate this triumph; rather, she intones an elegy over the dying myth of the heroic Innocent, over the days that are no more.

The Strength of Women and the Weakness of Men

Susan J. Rosowski

Some critics have faulted *My Ántonia* for its apparent lack of structure and the fact that the novel becomes Jim Burden's story at the expense of Ántonia Shimerda. Susan J. Rosowski argues that *My Ántonia* has a classic romantic structure, and that Cather's narrative technique explores male romanticism. Jim, who becomes the somewhat dissatisfied, seeking subject of *My Ántonia*, essentially turns Ántonia into a symbol, or object, that represents what he feels is best about life on the American frontier. While Jim needs this illusion to keep his memories of his childhood intact, he overlooks and loses all sense of Ántonia's uniqueness as an individual. Cather allows readers to see what Jim cannot: that Ántonia, like Lena Lingard and Tiny Soderball, is a fiercely independent woman who has always known what she has wanted. As a result, she has defied all expectations of her, including Jim's, and has succeeded admirably on her own terms. In contrast to Ántonia's independent, female strength is Jim's futile search for a past that will make his present life bearable. Susan J. Rosowski is a professor of English at the University of Nebraska. A prominent Cather scholar, she is the author of *The Voyage Perilous: Willa Cather's Romanticism* (1986) and the editor of *Approaches to Teaching Cather's* My Ántonia (1989).

One sign of Cather's achievement is that *My Ántonia* defies analysis, a quality critics often note when beginning a discussion of it. In 1918 W.C. Brownell said he did not "mind being incoherent" in writing of Cather's new book if he could "convey his notion in the least by [his] flounderings," compared its air to that of Homer, who lifted his subject "somehow," then concluded, "I don't know any art more essentially elusive." Half a century later James Woodress wrote of the same quality in different terms. *My Ántonia* has passion, and though "one knows when he is in the presence of it, . . . the identification of it is somewhat intuitive. . . . it is difficult to explain." More specific readings differ dramatically—David Stouck interprets it as a pastoral and Paul A. Olson as an epic; James E. Miller, Jr., as a commentary on the American dream and Blanche H. Gelfant as a drama of distorted sexuality—until one wonders how a single work can mean so many things to so many people. Yet the greatness of the book lies in precisely this capacity. With *My Ántonia* Cather introduced into American fiction what [Romantic poet] Wordsworth had introduced to English poetry a century earlier—the continuously changing work.

THE ROMANTIC STRUCTURE OF *MY ÁNTONIA*

By creating a narrator, Jim Burden, to recall Ántonia, a girl he knew while growing up in Nebraska, Cather for the first time in a novel used the narrative structure ideally suited to the romantic. She made the reacting mind a structural feature of her book. She then provided what [biographer] E.K. Brown called a "very curious preface," in which she instructed her reader about what was to follow. In that preface Cather anticipated major questions raised by critics. Is *My Ántonia* about Jim or about Ántonia? The question assumes mutually exclusive alternatives Cather rejected. Jim originally titled his story simply "Ántonia," then frowned, added "my," and seemed satisfied. As his title indicates, *My Ántonia* is about neither Jim nor Ántonia per se, but how the two, mind and object, come together, so "this girl seemed to mean to us the country, the conditions, the whole adventure of our childhood."

Is it a novel, and has it any form? The impetus for Jim's story was his desire to recollect his emotions, so that he might understand the pattern that emerges from them. To speak Ántonia's name "was to call up pictures of people and places, to set a quiet drama going in one's brain," and in writing, Jim was true to his experience of remembering. He didn't make notes, didn't arrange or rearrange, but "simply wrote down what of herself and myself and other people

Ántonia's name recalls to me." Thus his story is not structured by situation, as novels usually are, but by one person's feelings, in the manner of a lyric. Its meaning is as personal as its form; Jim specifies that his story won't be his reader's. When he presents his manuscript to Cather (and implicitly to each reader), he asks, "Now what about yours?" then cautions, "Don't let it influence your own story." This is a book, then, that hasn't a settled form, but instead that sets in motion an ever changing, expanding process of symbolic experience, "a quiet drama" in the mind of each reader.

That is not to say *My Ántonia* is formless. From the apparently episodic looseness of Jim's recollections emerges the classic romantic pattern of a dialectic between subject and object, momentarily resolved as a symbol. It consists of two major movements, followed by fusion: first, awakening to experience (Part I) and moving outward by its physicality (Part II), then awakening to ideas (Part III) and returning by them (Part IV); finally, fusing the two as symbol (Part V). By turning back upon itself, the pattern forms circles of expanding meaning. As Jim returned to scenes of his childhood, so the story returns the reader to the beginning, to recognize as symbols particulars once seen discretely. This is precisely the process Jim articulates at the conclusion (a misnomer, for here there is no conclusion, meaning is open-ended and ongoing), when he walks again along the first road over which he and Ántonia came together and realizes that man's experience is "a little circle.". . .

CATHER'S SUBVERSION OF TRADITIONAL ROMANTICISM

The overall pattern of *My Ántonia*, with its separation, resolution, and return to separation, is familiar to readers of Romantic literature: one need think only of Wordsworth's "Tintern Abbey," Coleridge's conversation poems, and Keats's odes. Like her predecessors in romanticism, Cather uses that pattern to write of the individual imagination perceiving the world symbolically. Unlike them, however, she uses gender assumptions to heighten tension between her subject and object. As her early essays make clear, Cather was acutely aware that our culture assigns to men the position of subject and to women that of object, and she incorporates those assumptions into her novel. Jim Burden expresses conventionally male attitudes: he assumes the subject position, moves outward, engages in change and progress, and writes possessively about *his* Ántonia as the archetypal woman who provides an anchorage for his travels and a muse for his imagination. Through Jim, Cather presents myths of male transcendence, of man as a liberating hero, romantic lover, and creative genius; of women to be rescued, loved, and transformed into art. In Ántonia, however, Cather contradicts these assumptions by creating a woman who works out her individual destiny in defiance of her narrator's expectations.

ÁNTONIA'S UNCONDITIONAL LOVE

My Ántonia is Jim's account of all that Ántonia means to him, or more precisely, of his youthful attempt to *make* her "anything that a woman can be to a man." By his account Ántonia seeks primarily to nurture by giving—to give her ring to the ten-year-old Jim and to admire his exploits, to give her love to Larry Donovan, and to give to her children a better chance than she had. As important, she makes no demands upon the world or upon others in it. Even after becoming pregnant, Ántonia does not press Larry Donovan to marry her, for "I thought if he saw how well I could do for him, he'd want to stay with me." Her husband, Cuzak, affirms "she is a good wife for a poor man" because "she don't ask me no questions." Ántonia offers unconditional love; both her strength and her weakness are that she could never believe harm of anyone she loved. Through her love, Ántonia, like the orchard she tends, offers "the deepest peace" of escape from worldly demands. To Jim, Ántonia is a wellspring for male activity in the larger world. On a physical level she bears sons. Jim titles his final chapter "Cuzak's Boys," and he concludes, "It was no wonder that her sons stood tall and straight." On a spiritual level she is a muse to Jim, for she "had that something which fires the imagination."

JIM'S UNCONDITIONAL LOVE

At the same time that Cather uses Jim to present "the collective myths" about women, she builds tension against his account. There emerges a certain ruthlessness about Jim's affection for Ántonia that belies his stated affection for her. His love, unlike hers, is conditional. He is proud of Ántonia when he believes her to be "like Snow-white, in the fairy tale"; he turns from her when she asserts her individuality. He resents her protecting manner toward him, is angered

over her masculine ways when she works the farm, is bitter
when she "throws herself away on . . . a cheap sort of fellow"
and, once pregnant, falls from social favor. Jim's allegiance
is consistently to his ideas; when they conflict with reality,
he denies the reality.

The world and the people in it just as consistently belie
the myths Jim attempts to impose upon them. Otto Fuchs is
not a Jesse James desperado but a warmhearted ranchhand;
Lena Lingard is not a wild seductress but a strong-minded
girl who becomes an independent businesswoman; Jim
himself is not the adventurer, the lover, or the poet he pre-
tends to be. By contrasting the boast and the deed, Cather
suggests comic, self-serving, and ineffectual dimensions of
male gallantry. Picturing himself as a dragon slayer, Jim
kills an old, lazy rattlesnake. Drafted by his grandmother
into service as Ántonia's rescuer, Jim sleeps at the Cutters,
saving Ántonia from rape but feeling something close to ha-
tred of her for embarrassing him. Resolving to "go home and
look after Ántonia," Jim returns to her only twenty years
later, after being assured that he will not have to part with
his illusions. Finally, Ántonia and Lena, the objects of Jim's
benevolence, react to his promise with smiles and "frank
amusement." They get on with their lives basically independently from men, whether by design, as when Lena resolves
that she will never marry, or by necessity, as when Ántonia
proceeds to rear her daughter alone.

Tension against Jim's account increases as his narrative
role changes. In the initial sections Cather presented Ántonia through Jim's point of view. Jim measured Ántonia
against his idea of women, approving of her when she assumed a role he expected of her. But in Book IV, "The Pioneer Woman's Story," Cather moved Jim aside, to the position of tale recorder, and made the midwife who attended
Ántonia the tale teller. The Widow Steavens provides a
woman's account of a woman's experience, and with it a significant change in tone toward Ántonia. She relates her story
with understanding and sympathy rather than with Jim's
shocked and bitter insistence that Ántonia play her part in
his myth.

THE REVERSAL OF ROLES

By Part V, Jim and Ántonia have reversed roles. Jim began
the novel as the storyteller in several senses, telling the ac-

count he titles *my* Ántonia, and also telling it in terms of stories he has read or heard—*The Life of Jesse James, Robinson
Crusoe, Camille,* the *Georgics.* But the child Jim grew into a
man who followed the most conventional pattern for success: he left the farm to move to town, then attended the university, studied law at Harvard, married well, and joined a
large corporation. In the process, his personal identity
seems to have faded. Ántonia, who began the novel as a
character rendered by Jim, in the fifth section breaks
through myths Jim had imposed upon her and emerges
powerfully as herself. With her children around her, she is
the center of "the family legend," to whom her children look
"for stories and entertainment." Ántonia's stories, unlike
Jim's, are not from literature. They are instead domestic
ones drawn from life, "about the calf that broke its leg, or
how Yulka saved her little turkeys from drowning . . . or
about old Christmases and weddings in Bohemia."

THE DESTRUCTION OF MALE MYTHS

As Jim leaves the Cuzak farm in the last paragraphs, Ántonia recedes into the background. One of a group standing by
the windmill, she is waving her apron, as countless women
have said good-bye to countless men. Returning to the larger
male world, Jim spends a disappointing day in Black Hawk,
talking idly with an old lawyer there. Finally, he walks outside of town to the unploughed prairie that remains from
early times. There Jim's mind "was full of pleasant things,"
for he intended "to play" with Cuzak's boys and, after the
boys are grown, "to tramp along a few miles of lighted
streets with Cuzak." But these plans seem curiously empty,
irrelevant to the center of life represented by the female
world of Ántonia. The early male myths of adventure have
led to pointless wandering and lonely exile, and the women,
originally assigned roles of passivity, have become the vital
sources of meaning.

CHAPTER 3

Character and Character Foils in *My Ántonia*

READINGS ON
MY ÁNTONIA

The Parallel and Divergent Paths of Jim and Ántonia

Wallace Stegner

In his classic essay on *My Ántonia,* Wallace Stegner proclaims the novel as an artistic triumph. Stegner maintains that the novel is best understood as a process by which its two major characters, Jim and Ántonia, meet and share vital experiences, and then gradually move apart as each pursues a very different life. With the reunion in the novel's final pages, their lives once again converge, and we see what for Cather constitutes true success. The path Jim chose led to his becoming a wealthy, highly regarded lawyer in New York, but he is incomplete and vaguely dissatisfied, unsure of who or what he is. Ántonia, however, by meeting her simplest needs and always knowing what she wants, has become something greater—"a rich mine of life" who mirrors the triumph of yielding abundance and fulfillment out of the harsh conditions of the Nebraska plains. Wallace Stegner (1909–1993) wrote many successful novels, including the Pulitzer Prize–winning *Angle of Repose* (1971) and *Crossing to Safety* (1987). His collection of essays *The American West as Living Space* (1987) examined the impact of the West on the American consciousness.

If, as is often said, every novelist is born to write one thing, then the one thing that Willa Cather was born to write was first fully realized in *My Ántonia* (1918). In that novel the people are the Bohemian and Swedish immigrants she had known in her childhood on the Nebraska plains; the prose is the prose of her maturity—flexible, evocative, already tend-

Excerpted from Wallace Stegner, *The American Novel: From James Fenimore Cooper to William Faulkner.* Copyright © 1965 Basic Books, Inc. Reprinted with permission from Perseus Books Group.

ing to a fastidious bareness but not yet gone pale and cool; the novelistic skill is of the highest, the structure at once free and intricately articulated; the characters stretch into symbolic suggestiveness as naturally as trees cast shadows in the long light of a prairie evening; the theme is the fully exposed, complexly understood theme of the American orphan or exile, struggling to find a place between an old world left behind and a new world not yet created.

But to say that Willa Cather found her subject and her manner and her theme in *My Ántonia* is not to say that she found them easily. When *My Ántonia* appeared, Miss Cather was forty-five years old. She had already had one career as a teacher and another as an editor, and she had published a good many short stories and three other novels.

The first of these, *Alexander's Bridge* (1911) was a nearly total mistake—a novel laid in London and dealing with the attenuated characters and fragile ethical problems of the genteel tradition. In writing it, Cather later remarked, she was trying to sing a song that did not lie in her voice. Urged by her friend Sarah Orne Jewett to try something closer to her own experience, she revived her Western memories with a trip to Arizona and New Mexico and, after her return to Pittsburgh,

> began to write a story entirely for myself; a story about some Scandinavians and Bohemians who had been neighbours of ours when I lived on a ranch in Nebraska, when I was eight or nine years old. I found it a much more absorbing occupation than writing *Alexander's Bridge;* a different process altogether. Here there was no arranging or "inventing"; everything was spontaneous and took its own place. . . . This was like taking a ride through familiar country on a horse that knew the way, on a fine morning when you felt like riding.

As she herself instantly recognized, that second book, *O Pioneers!* (1913), came close to being the tune that "lay in her voice." She wrote it spontaneously because she was tapping both memory and affection. She thought of the subject matter as a considerable innovation, because no American writer had yet used Swedish immigrants for any but comic purposes, and nobody had ever written about Nebraska, considered in literary circles the absolute home of the clodhopper. Actually, there was nothing so revolutionary about the subject matter—it was merely one further extension of the local-color curiosity about little-known places and picturesque local types. Hamlin Garland had done German and

Norwegian immigrants very like these, on Wisconsin and Iowa farms very like Miss Cather's Nebraska ones, in *Main-Travelled Roads* (1891). *O Pioneers!* was new in its particulars, but not new in type, and it was not Willa Cather's fully trained voice that was heard in it. In its method, the book is orthodox; the heroine, Alexandra Bergson, is a type of earth goddess; the theme is the theme of the conquest of a hard country that had dominated novels of the American settlement ever since James Fenimore Cooper's *The Pioneers* in 1823. Miss Cather's novel, in fact, is considerably slighter and simpler than Cooper's of similar title.

In her third book, *The Song of the Lark* (1915), we can see Miss Cather systematically and consciously working for the enlargement and complication of her theme. The locale, at least in the beginning, is again Nebraska, though she calls it Colorado; the chief character is again a local girl of immigrant parentage, great promise, and few advantages. But the antagonist here is not the earth, and triumph is nothing so simple as the hewing of a farm out of a hard country. To the problem of survival has been added the problem of culture. The struggle is involved with the training of Thea Kronborg's fine voice; the effort of the novel is to explore how a talent may find expression even when it appears in a crude little railroad town on the plains, and how a frontier American may lift himself from his traditionless, artless environment to full stature as an artist and an individual.

NEW WORLD VERSUS OLD

Here we see developing the dynamism between old world and new that occurs strongly again not only in *My Ántonia* but in *One of Ours* (1922), *The Professor's House* (1925), *Death Comes for the Archbishop* (1927), *Shadows on the Rock* (1931), and several of the short stories such as "Neighbor Rosicky." It is as if Miss Cather conceived the settlement of her country as a marriage between a simple, fresh, hopeful young girl and a charming, worldly, but older man. Thea Kronborg's German music teacher, Herr Wunsch, is the first of those cultivated and unhappy Europeans who people Miss Cather's fictions—exiles who, though doomed themselves by the hardships of pioneering, pass on sources of life and art to the eager young of a new land. Thea, like Alexandra Bergson before her and Ántonia Shimerda later, is that best sort of second-generation American who learns or retains some of the intellectual and artistic tradition of Europe without losing the American freshness and without falling into the common trap of a commercial and limited "practicality." These are all success stories of sorts, and all reflect a very American groping toward a secure identity.

But even *The Song of the Lark* was not the precise song that lay in Willa Cather's voice. Or rather, it was the right tune, but she sang it imperfectly. The story of Thea Kronborg's struggle to become an opera singer is told with a realism so detailed that it is exhausting; and it ended by offending its author nearly as much as the pretentiousness of *Alexander's Bridge*. "Too much detail," she concluded later, "is apt, like any form of extravagance, to become slightly vulgar." She never tried a second time the "full-blooded method": When the next book came along, "quite of itself, and with no direction from me, it took the road of *O Pioneers!*—not the road of *The Song of the Lark*."

THE TRIUMPH OF *MY ÁNTONIA*

The next one was, of course, *My Ántonia*. But the road it took was not quite exactly that of *O Pioneers!* For though the place is still Nebraska and the protagonist is still an immigrant girl contending with the handicaps of a physical and emotional transplanting, *My Ántonia* is a major novel where the earlier ones were trial efforts. *O Pioneers!* was truly simple; *My Ántonia* only looks simple. *The Song of the Lark* was cluttered in its attempt to deal with complexity; *My Ántonia* gives complexity the clean lines and suggestive subtlety of fine architecture.

One technical device which is fundamental to the greater concentration and suggestiveness of *My Ántonia* is the point of view from which it is told. Both of the earlier "Nebraska novels" had been reported over the protagonist's shoulder, with omniscient intrusions by the author. Here the whole story is told by a narrator, Jim Burden, a boyhood friend of Ántonia, later a lawyer representing the railroads. The use of the narrative mask permits Miss Cather to exercise her sensibility without obvious self-indulgence: Burden becomes an instrument of the selectivity that she worked for. He also permits the easy condensation and syncopation of time—an indispensable technical tool in a novel that covers more than thirty years and deals in a complex way with a theme of development. Finally, Jim Burden is used constantly as a suggestive parallel to Ántonia: he is himself an orphan and has been himself transplanted (from the East, from Virginia), and is himself groping for an identity and an affiliation. In the process of understanding and commemorating Ántonia, he locates himself; we see the essential theme from two points, and the space between those points serves as a base line for triangulation.

THE PARALLEL PATHS OF JIM AND ÁNTONIA

The parallel is stressed from the beginning, when Jim, an orphan of ten, arrives in Black Hawk, Nebraska, on his way to live with his grandparents, and sees the immigrant Shimerda family huddling in bewilderment on the station platform, speaking their strange lost tongue. As he is driven to the ranch under a great unfamiliar sky, across a land that planes off mysteriously into darkness—"not a country, but the material out of which countries are made"—Jim feels so lost and strange and uprooted that he cannot even say the prayers that have been taught him back in Virginia. "Between that earth and sky I felt erased, blotted out."

For Jim, protected by his relatives, the strangeness soon wears away. For the Shimerdas, who have none of the tools or skills of farmers, no friends, no English, and who discover that the land they have been sold is bad and their house a sod cave, transplanting is a harsher trial, and harder on the old than on the young, and on the sensitive than on the dull. With the help of their neighbors the Burdens, the Shimerdas make a beginning, but before their first Christmas in the new land Papa Shimerda, gentle, helpless, homesick for the old life in Prague, has killed himself with a shotgun. Survival, which Miss Cather presents as a process of inevitable brutalization, is best managed by the grasping Mama Shimerda and her sullen son Ambroz. The fourteen-year-old girl, Ántonia, pretty and intelligent and her father's darling, must put off any hope of schooling and become one of the breadwinners for her miserably poor family. The deprivation is symbolic: this is the deculturation enforced on the frontier. The one thing beautiful in her life, the thing she shares with Jim, is the land itself, the great sea of grass, the wild roses in the fence corners of spring, the mighty weathers, and the tiny things—insects and flowers and little animals—that the eye notices because on the plains there is so little else to take the attention.

Ántonia and Jim as children share a kind of Eden, but they are going toward different futures. At the end of the first long section, which is divided between the presentation of the hardships of an immigrant family and Miss Cather's delicate nostalgic evocation of the freedom and beauty of the untamed land, Jim and Ántonia are lying together on top of the Burdens' chicken house while a great electrical storm comes on and "the felty beat of raindrops" begins in the dust. Why, Jim asks her, can't she always be "nice, like this"? Why must she all the time try to be like her brother Ambroz? "If I live here like you," Ántonia says, "that is different. Things will be easy for you. But they will be hard for us."

There are gradations in the penalties of exile; the most violently uprooted have the least chance. Section Two of the novel reinforces this idea by moving the action from the half-idyllic country to the limited and restricting little town of Black Hawk. In pages that forecast some of the attitudes of Sinclair Lewis' *Main Street* (1920), Miss Cather reveals the pettiness and snobbery, the vulgar commercialism, the cultural starvation, the forming class distinctions, the pathetic pleasures of a typical prairie town just beyond the pioneering stage. Ántonia, Lena Lingard, Tiny Soderball, and other Bohemian, Norwegian, and Swedish immigrant girls work as servants in the houses of the so-called "better families," and though they are snubbed by the town girls they demonstrate in their vitality and health something sturdier and more admirable than the more advantaged can show. Those for whom "things are easy" develop less character than these girls deprived of school, forced to work at menial jobs, dedicating their wages to help their families back on the farm. They do not even know that Black Hawk is a deprived little hole, but throw themselves wholeheartedly into the town dances and into any pleasure and excitement their world affords. Miss Cather sums up both desire and deprivation in a brief winter scene:

> In the winter bleakness a hunger for colour came over people, like the Laplander's craving for fats and sugar. Without knowing why, we used to linger on the sidewalk outside the church when the lamps were lighted early for choir practice or prayer-meeting, shivering and talking until our feet were like lumps of ice. The crude reds and greens and blues of that coloured glass held us there.

It is Jim Burden speaking, but he speaks even more for the "hired girls" than for himself, for he is not confined within Black Hawk's limitations as they are. For him there is more than crude colored glass; opportunity opens outward to the state university in the city of Lincoln. For Ántonia and the others there is only housework, the amorous advances of people like Wick Cutter, the town money-lender, and the probability that eventually they will marry some farmer of their own immigrant background, who will work them like farm horses.

Part Three of *My Ántonia* has been objected to as a structural mistake, because it turns away from Ántonia and focuses on the university and city life of Jim Burden—on the opening of his mind, the passionate response he makes to books and ideas under the tutelage of a favorite professor, the quiet affair he has with Lena Lingard, who has set up in the city as a dressmaker. But the criticism seems based on too simplistic a view of the novel's intention. Though the title suggests that Ántonia is the focus of the book, the development from the symbolic beginning scene is traced through both Ántonia and Jim, and a good part of that theme of development is concerned with the possible responses to deprivation and to opportunity. We leave Ántonia in Book Three in order to return to her with more understanding later.

A high point of Jim's life in Lincoln is a performance of *Camille* that he and Lena Lingard attend. Like so many of Miss Cather's scenes, it expands effortlessly out of the particular and into the symbolic. The performance is shabby, the actors are broken-down, but to Jim the play is magic. Its bright illusion concentrates for him everything that he hopes for as he starts east to Harvard to continue his studies, going farther from his country, back toward the intellectual and artistic things that his country has left behind or possesses only in second-rate and vulgarized forms. It is worth observing that Jim Burden leaves Nebraska on a note of illusion.

Section Four returns us to Ántonia and to Black Hawk. Back after two years at Harvard, Jim hears that in his absence Ántonia has eloped with a railroad conductor and that after being deceived and abandoned she has returned to her brother Ambroz's farm to bear her child and work in the fields like a man. The contrast between her pitiful failure and Jim's growing opportunities is deliberate; so is the trick of letting Jim come back to Ántonia little by little, first through the stories told of her by townspeople and only later in person. When he does finally go to the farm to see her, the deliberate structural split that began with Book Three is finally mended. Their lives will continue to run in different channels, but they have rediscovered the "old times" that they have in common, the things that by now Ántonia could not bear to leave. "I like to be where I know every stack and tree, and where all the ground is friendly," she says. Her bond is with the land—she all but *is* the land—while Jim will go on to law school and to occupations and associations unimaginable to her. Again Miss Cather catches a significant moment in a reverberating image, to show both the difference and the intimate relationship between these two:

> As we walked homeward across the fields, the sun dropped and lay like a great golden globe in the low west. While it hung there, the moon rose in the east, as big as a cart-wheel, pale silver and streaked with rose colour, thin as a bubble or a ghost-moon. For five, perhaps ten minutes, the two luminaries confronted each other across the level land, resting on opposite edges of the world.

"I'll come back," Jim says, leaving Ántonia, and she replies, "Perhaps you will. But even if you don't, you're here, like my father." Because we must give scenes like these more than realistic value, we recognize here an insistence, not only on the shared beauty of childhood in the new land, but on the other tradition that is going to go on operating in Ántonia's life, the gift of her father with his gentleness and his taste. In Ántonia, new world and old world, nature and nurture, meet as they meet in Jim, in different proportions and with different emphasis.

ÁNTONIA'S TRIUMPH AND JIM'S "BURDEN"

That union of two worlds is made explicit in Book Five, when twenty years later Jim Burden returns again to Nebraska and finds Ántonia married to an amiable, half-successful Bohemian farmer, with a brood of healthy boys. She is no longer an eager girl, but a worn woman. But the same warmth of spirit still glows in her, and her life that had been half-wrecked has been put back together. In most ways, hers is an American family; but within the family they speak only Czech, and thus something of Papa Shimerda, something of Bohemia, is kept—something related to those strangenesses that Jim Burden had noted as a small boy: the dry brown chips he saw the Shimerdas nibbling, that were dried mushrooms picked in some far-off Bohemian forest; and the way Mama Shimerda, given title to a cow by Jim's grandfather, seized his hand in a totally un-American gesture and kissed it. A partly remembered but valued tradition and an empty land have fused and begun to be something new.

As for Jim Burden, we understand at last that the name Willa Cather chose for him was not picked by accident. For Jim not only, as narrator, carries the "burden" or tune of the novel; he carries also the cultural burden that Willa Cather herself carried, the quintessentially American burden of re-making in the terms of a new place everything that makes life graceful and civilized. To become a European or an easterner is only to reverse and double the exile. The education that lured Jim Burden away from Nebraska had divided him against himself, as Willa Cather was divided. Like people, the education that comes from elsewhere must be modified to fit a new environment. In becoming a man of the world, Jim Burden discovers that he has almost forgotten to be a man from Nebraska. It is Ántonia, who now achieves some of the quality of earth goddess that Alexandra Bergson had in *O Pioneers!,* who reminds him that no matter where his mind has been, his heart has always been here.

Jim Burden at the end of the novel is in the same position that Willa Cather was in when she finally found the people and themes and country that she was "born to write." The final paragraph is like the closing of a door, shutting in things that until now have been exposed or scattered. As Jim walks through the country he stumbles upon a stretch of the old pioneer wagon road of his childhood:

> This was the road over which Ántonia and I came on the night when we got off the train at Black Hawk and were bedded down in the straw, wondering children, being taken we knew not whither. I had only to close my eyes to hear the rumbling of the wagons in the dark, and to be again overcome by that obliterating strangeness. The feelings of that night were so near that I could reach out and touch them with my hand. I had the sense of coming home to myself, and of having found out what a little circle man's experience is. For Ántonia and for me, this had been the road of Destiny; had taken us to those early accidents of fortune which predetermined for us all that we can ever be. Now I understand that the same road was to bring us together again. Whatever we had missed, we possessed together the precious, the incommunicable past.

WILLA CATHER AND JIM BURDEN

It is difficult not to hear in that passage the voice of Willa Cather, who like Jim left raw Nebraska to become a citizen of the world, and like him was drawn back. Jim Burden is more than a narrative device: he is an essential part of the theme, a demonstration of how such an American may reconcile the two halves of himself. And Ántonia is more than a woman and a character. Jim describes her toward the end as "a rich mine of life, like the founders of early races." Miss Cather, who did not believe in laboring a point any more than she believed in overfurnishing a novel, clearly wanted us to take away that image of Ántonia. A mine of life, the mother of races, a new thing forming itself in hardship and hope, but clinging to fragments of the well-loved old. Hence *My Ántonia*—any American's Ántonia, Willa Cather's Ántonia. No writer ever posed that essential aspect of the American experience more warmly, with more nostalgic lyricism, or with a surer understanding of what it means.

The Land and Ántonia Shimerda Are Fused into One

Mary Kemper Sternshein

Often a novel's setting serves no other purpose beyond its role as a backdrop for more important elements such as plot and character development. Mary Kemper Sternshein maintains that the setting of *My Ántonia* is an important exception. For Sternshein, rural Nebraska becomes a character in and of itself, and Cather presents the changing seasons and the development of the unbroken land in concert with Ántonia's growth as a character. By the novel's end, Cather has established Ántonia as an earth mother— a rich representation of the promise and fulfillment of settlement on the frontier. A teacher and librarian, Mary Kemper Sternshein has written about Willa Cather, the American West, and Middle English.

Setting is a necessary element of any novel, but only a few authors have made a Great Plains setting an integral part of their stories. The Great Plains setting of novels has served mainly as a backdrop. This backdrop is lowered into place in the first chapter of the book and remains there throughout the novel without becoming obtrusive or interfering with the plot. When used like this, the Great Plains setting never becomes a part of the novel. None of the features of the land are worked into the novel, so the reader is never aware of the changes in the land or the seasons' coming and going. Setting is as automatic as capitalizing the first letter of the first word of a sentence—it is done as a matter of course and then forgotten.

THE INTERMINGLING OF LAND AND CHARACTER

Not all authors are guilty of this sin of omission. Willa Cather, in her novel *My Ántonia*, chooses the Nebraska ter-

Reprinted from Mary Kemper Sternshein, "The Land of Nebraska and Ántonia Shimerda," *Heritage of the Great Plains*, 16:2, Spring 1983. Reprinted with permission from the Center for Great Plains Studies.

ritory as her setting. She does not stop with that choice. As the novel progresses, the land plays an important part, perhaps the most important part, of the story. The land is as important as any of the characters in the novel. To illustrate this point, land, images of the earth, plowing, harvesting, the cycle of the seasons are used in the novel *My Ántonia* by Willa Cather to parallel the growth and development of Ántonia Shimerda, one of the characters.

The land of Nebraska is revealed to us through the eyes of Jim Burden. He sees Nebraska after dark as he rides to his grandparents' home in a wagon. The only land to which Jim can compare this new territory is his old home, Virginia. Jim notices immediately that there are no mountains here—only land and sky. As a matter of fact, after more thought, Jim decides

> There was nothing but land: not a country at all, but the material out of which countries are made. . . . I had the feeling that the world was left behind, that we had got over the edge of it, and were outside man's jurisdiction. . . . Between that earth and that sky I felt erased, blotted out.

When Jim goes to bed, he doesn't say his prayers because he is still awed by the magnitude of this new country. He's even a little frightened by its size.

The following morning, Jim's feelings completely change. The light of day helps to make this new country familiar and inviting. Jim now sees

> . . . that the grass was the country, as the water is the sea. The red of the grass made all the great prairie the colour of wine-stains, or of certain seaweeds when they are first washed up. And there was so much motion in it; the whole country, seemed, somehow, to be running.

Thus, the very things which bothered Jim the previous night in the dark on the way to his new home now delight him. He does not mind the absence of the mountains—he notices the grass and how it blows in the wind resembling waves. The waves of grass are moving so swiftly that they seem to run; they are free. Jim describes other parts of the country as having this feeling of freedom. Once he says "The road ran like a wild thing. . . ." Later he feels that ". . . sunflower-bordered roads always seem to me the roads to freedom." All of Jim's observations point to one thing. Human beings have not made much of a mark on the frontier of Nebraska. Jim does not include in his descriptions acre after acre of cultivated fields or wooden A-frame houses. The Burdens have the only wooden house. The other houses are made of sod. The roads are not paved; they're not even graveled. Dirt roads snake from one farm house to the next. The country seems almost as young as Jim.

Jim isn't the only newcomer to the country of Nebraska. Ántonia Shimerda comes to Nebraska with her family. We first hear of Ántonia while Jim is traveling on the train. The conductor tells Jim about a young girl who can not speak English. We assume that she is foreign. The conductor continues to kid Jim about the girl who is "as bright as a new dollar."

"Don't you want to go ahead and see her, Jimmy? She's got the pretty brown eyes, too!"

This last remark made me bashful.

When Jim first sees Ántonia, she is "clutching an oilcloth bundle." Once again, Jim pushes this disturbing idea—a girl—into the back of his mind. He was not impressed after his first meeting with her. She was different from any other girl he had met.

The Burdens paid a neighborly visit to the Shimerdas, where Jim meets Ántonia formally this time. In the daytime, Jim notices that Ántonia is actually pretty. She does have big eyes; they are also brown and full of light like the sun. Ántonia runs up to Jim, coaxingly holds out her hand, and runs up the hill. Ántonia laughs as her skirt blows in the wind. After she, Jim, and Yulka have their first English lesson there on the hill, Ántonia impulsively gives Jim her ring.

JIM, ÁNTONIA, AND THE LAND

It is easy to see, within the first few pages of the novel, how the country of Nebraska and Ántonia are similarly described. Both instill a feeling of apprehension in Jim when he sees them for the first time in the dark. When seen in the sunlight, both Nebraska and Ántonia have beautiful qualities. They are both free and uncontrolled. They are both impulsive and untamed, yet they are generous, also.

Nebraska is not always this inviting and friendly to people. In winter, the entire country freezes solid. It is barren of all forms of life. Snow is everywhere, and it often drifts up and around the houses; an act which necessitates tunneling out. Winter in Nebraska isn't cruel or mean, but it is hard and bitter.

Winter comes down savagely over a little town on the prairie. The wind that sweeps in from the open country strips away all the leafy screens that hide one yard from another in summer, and the houses seem to draw closer together. . . . The pale, cold light of the winter sunset did not beautify—it was like the light of truth itself. When the smoky clouds hung low in the west and the red sun went down behind them, leaving a pink flush on the snowy roofs and the blue drifts, then the wind sprang up afresh, with a kind of bitter song, as if it said: 'This is reality, whether you like it or not. All those frivolities of summer, the light and shadow, the living mask of green that trembled over everything, they were lies, and this is what was underneath. This is the truth.' It was as if we were being punished for loving the loveliness of summer.

Many times families were cut off from town or from neighbors for months. Individual families must manage on their own. They must be resourceful enough to keep morale high and to make the best of the situation. The Shimerda family does not have this resourcefulness necessary to survive intact through the winter. Mr. Shimerda, Ántonia's beloved father, commits suicide shortly after Christmas. Following her father's death and subsequent funeral, Ántonia could, herself, turn bitter toward life. As signs of spring appear on the Nebraska prairie, Ántonia becomes more reconciled to her father's death.

Spring bounces in like a new puppy. The Shimerdas "spring clean" and alleviate many of their uncomfortable problems. They have a new four-room cabin, a windmill, a hen house, and chickens. They even have a milk cow. Their fields are ready to be planted. Ántonia still retains her tendency to respond to questions in a sharp and biting manner. She pumps Jim for information about planting corn and then very rudely insults his grandfather. She very haughtily remarks that Jim's grandfather is not Jesus. He doesn't know everything. As winter finally melts into spring, most of these cutting remarks melt from Ántonia's mind and another season approaches.

THE FLOWERING OF THE LAND AND ÁNTONIA'S EMERGING ADULTHOOD

As spring advances into summer, Ántonia and the land of Nebraska become even closer together. Ántonia has accepted her father's death, but she knows that he killed himself partially because the country was too inhospitable to him. It was not cultivated as he was. Ántonia begins to work the land with a vengeance. She does not go to school like the other children in the territory do. She stays home and works "like mans." She runs her own team of oxen and works just as long and hard as her brother does to cultivate this wild, free land. She does regret her inability to go to school because Jim catches her crying on the way to the barn one day. Even though her father has instilled in her a strong desire for education, she somehow knows that the land must be tamed before time can be spent with trivialities and extras like school. The death of Ántonia's father also killed the civilized, educated facet of the Shimerda family. When Ántonia begins to work in the fields like a man, her "civilized attributes wither away." Her genteel manners and social veneer are stripped away, leaving a woman just as coarse and crude as any male field hand. Thus, as the land of Nebraska is being stripped of the red grass by the plow, Ántonia is also being stripped of her initial attributes as she works in the fields.

When Ántonia moves to town as a hired girl, she loses much of her contact with the land. Of all the seasons discussed during Ántonia's stay in town, winter is most predominant. Even Jim notices that winter in town is different than winter on the farm.

> Winter lies too long in country towns; hangs on until it is stale and shabby, old and sullen. On the farm the weather was the great fact, and men's affairs went on underneath it, as the streams creep under the ice. But in Black Hawk the scene of human life was spread out shrunken and pinched, frozen down to the bare stalk.

The winter drags in town. There is nothing to do to relieve the monotony as there was on the farm. All the young people of Black Hawk become involved with music and dancing at the dancing pavilion. Ántonia especially enjoys dancing and tries to go to the pavilion as often as she can. She has "relearned" her civilized social manners while she works at the Harlings. Her intense joy of dancing helps her to lose her job with the Harling family. Her ability to enjoy herself in the dancing pavilion also begins to change her reputation slightly. In the winter in a city, people need diversion. Ántonia becomes a diversion. All of the city boys like to dance with her, yet they know and she knows that no serious relationship will develop.

Only once during her stay in Black Hawk does Ántonia ever revert back to the feelings and thoughts she had when she was young. Ántonia and two other girls are in the country picking wild flowers. They meet Jim there. Jim notices that Ántonia has been crying. The flowers have made her homesick; her homesickness has made her miss her father. She reminisces for a few minutes and then asks Jim about her father's spirit once more. Jim reassures her that her father's spirit is happy. Then, amid the spring blossoms, the new green leaves, the butterflies, bees, and singing birds, Jim reflects that "Ántonia seemed to me that day exactly like the little girl who used to come to our house with Mr. Shimerda." In this springtime setting, "Ántonia had the most trusting, responsive eyes in the world; love and credulousness seemed to look out of them with open faces." When Lena Lingard interrupts Ántonia's solitude and reminiscing, Ántonia returns once again to the gay, carefree hired girl on an outing picking wild flowers. The weather subtly changes, too. It becomes hot; almost unbearably hot. The heat was so great "that the dogwoods and scrub oaks began to turn up the silvery underside of their leaves, and all the foliage looked soft and wilted." The attitudes of both Ántonia and the weather have changed, however subtly, when reminded of the present.

The very last thing that Ántonia, Jim, and their friends see that day is an ordinary plough standing alone in a field. The vision is beautiful. The plough entirely fills the red-orange circle of the sun. Jim describes the picture.

> Magnified across the distance by the horizontal light, it stood out against the sun, was exactly contained within the circle of the disk; the handles, the tongue, the share—black against the molten red. There it was, heroic in size, a picture writing on the sun.

The plough stands for more than the material object it represents. It is a symbol of a whole way of life; it stands for a settled agricultural civilization. Human beings are beginning to conquer and tame the country of Nebraska. Seeing ploughs and cultivated fields is more common than seeing the red grass which grew on the prairie. The cultivation process is not nearly complete at this point, though, just as Ántonia's new-found manners do not do her any good until she begins to use them in her favor.

FURTHER PARALLELS BETWEEN ÁNTONIA AND THE LAND

A large break in time separates us from Ántonia and Jim. Jim leaves Nebraska, finds a job in the East, and marries.

When he returns to Black Hawk years later, he comes during a hot summer. He has been somewhat disillusioned by life, and he has returned to Nebraska to revive and to relive memories of things he thought were important. He hears the story of Ántonia's child from Mrs. Steavens. Ántonia packed to leave Nebraska for Denver one day in March. It was a raw, cold day, and it was raining. Ántonia herself fluctuated between being happy at the news and sad about leaving the country for good. When Ántonia returns to her family disgraced, the weather once again foreshadows her future. When she arrived, "It was one of them lovely warm May days, and the wind was blowing and the colts jumping around in the pastures. . . ." For the remainder of the summer and the fall, Ántonia works in the fields, plows, and tends livestock. The weather remains mild and calm just as Ántonia remains quiet and steady. Ántonia no longer "puts on airs" or brags about anything. She suffers through pain quietly by herself. She only goes to town when it is unavoidable. Summer and fall are placid times.

Ántonia's next incident is also foreshadowed by the weather. A heavy snowstorm falls as Ántonia struggles to drive her cattle home. This is the third heavy snow in the book. During the first, Mr. Shimerda shot himself. During the second heavy snow when Jim and Ántonia lived in Black Hawk, Ántonia begins dancing with the young men in town and creates a reputation different from the one she maintained while living on the farm. During this third storm, Ántonia's child is born. Mrs. Steavens stops her story at this point, and the next morning, Jim meets Ántonia once again out in the fields on the farm. The season is summer. The day is hot. As the sun sets, the moon vies for brilliancy in the sky.

> In that singular light every little tree and shock of wheat, every sunflower stalk and clump of snow-on-the-mountain, drew itself up high and pointed; the very clods and furrows in the fields seemed to stand up sharply. I felt the old pull of the earth, the solemn magic that comes out of those fields at nightfall.

Ántonia and the land of Nebraska are once again paralleled. After having her child, Ántonia decides to stay on the farm and work the land. As she plants corn, plows, tends livestock, etc., she begins to regain her self-esteem and self-confidence. She's ready to pick up where she left off years ago and make the best of her life. In this respect, the land is doing the same thing. The plants are standing tall and straight, high and pointed. Regardless of the size of the plant, each is striving to reach as high as it can. With an atmosphere like this created at the end of Book Four, the reader feels optimistic about Book Five. He hopes that Ántonia will remain content and stable since she has returned to a life she loves and knows well.

We don't see Ántonia again for twenty years. As Jim walks through her yard to the house, this is the view he sees.

> . . . the forest of tall hollyhocks. . . . The front yard was enclosed by a thorny locust hedge, and at the gate grew two silvery, mothlike trees of the mimosa family. From here one looked down over the cattle-yards, with their two long ponds, and over a wide stretch of stubble which they told me was a ryefield in summer. . . . Behind the houses were an ash grove and two orchards: a cherry orchard, with gooseberry and currant bushes between the rows, and an apple orchard, sheltered by a high hedge from the hot winds.

THE LAND AND THE AMERICAN DREAM

Jim seems slightly surprised at finding so much cultivation of the land. He is also mildly surprised at the number of children Ántonia has had. Both the land and Ántonia have been bountiful and produced well after they were "tamed." Neither the land nor Ántonia's spirit will ever be truly conquered, but both have been tamed enough to be malleable. Ántonia and the land are so much a part of each other now that it would not be inappropriate to classify Ántonia as an earth mother. Everything she does becomes fruitful and multiplies. Jim even says:

> She was a battered woman now, not a lovely girl; but she still had that something which fires the imagination, could still stop one's breath for a moment by a look or gesture that somehow revealed the meaning in common things. She had only to stand in the orchard, to put her hand on a little crab tree and look up at the apples, to make you feel the goodness of planting and tending and harvesting at last.

Ántonia herself has realized how important the land is to her. She commented on this occasionally throughout the book, but only after the birth of her first child does she really feel a close bond to the land. She comments that she could never live in a city because

> I like to be where I know every stack and tree, and where all the ground is friendly.

"I belong on a farm. I'm never lonesome here like I used to be in town. You remember what sad spells I used to have, when I didn't know what was the matter with me? I've never had them out here. Ántonia is content with her life; she no longer fights against it or tries to find pleasure elsewhere. She has helped to cultivate and tame the land so that her children may now engage in the frivolities of education, music, and other fields in the humanities.

The reader should never believe that the spirits of the land or of Ántonia have been dampened or destroyed. The indomitable, wild, free spirits both exist at the end of the novel. There is one spot of land that has never been cultivated and never will be. The red grass of Nebraska still grows there, wild and free. Mr. Shimerda's grave is this spot. Jim described it well.

> . . . instinctively we walked toward that unploughed patch at the crossing of the roads as the fittest place to talk to each other. . . . The tall red grass had never been cut there. It had died down in winter and come up again in the spring until it was as thick and shrubby as some tropical garden-grass.

Ántonia also has preserved her wild and free spirit, but she has done so in a slightly different manner. Leo, her twelve year old son, represents this freedom of mind and spirit. Leo is as Ántonia was when she first came to Nebraska. Ántonia says of him "That Leo; he's the worst of all. . . . And I love him the best. . . ." He is a mischievous little boy who enjoys almost everything—especially being alive. Leo is also the one child of Ántonia's who represents Mr. Shimerda's artistry. Leo is the person who plays his grandfather's old violin. Even Leo's description is one conducive to wild freedom. Jim says

> . . . he really was faun-like. He hadn't much head behind his ears, and his tawny fleece grew down thick to the back of his neck. His eyes were not frank and wide apart like those of the other boys, but were deep-set, gold-green in colour, and seemed sensitive to the light.

Jim's description goes even further, though, and tells us of Leo's innermost thoughts. When Leo wakes up before the rest of the family, Jim thinks,

> He seemed conscious of possessing a keener power of enjoyment than other people; his quick recognitions made him frantically impatient of deliberate judgments. He always knew what he wanted without thinking.

Leo, then, typifies the person Ántonia was as a child. He will have the opportunities Ántonia did not have. Leo can pursue any desire he wishes.

The novel ends at this point, after having securely tied the ends of the story together. Ántonia is finally seen as an earth mother; she and the earth become synonymous with each other. They eventually compliment each other and serve the same function. Although both the land and Ántonia are "tamed" by their experiences with life, neither has lost a strong sense of freedom. The novel ends on this note. The feeling of wildness and freedom will never be taken away from either the land or from Ántonia's family. They are too much a part of each other.

Black Hawk: A Foil for *My Ántonia*'s Characters

Anthony Channell Hilfer

Anthony Channell Hilfer believes that *My Ántonia* fails to create distinct, complex characters to whom readers can fully respond. He attributes this failure to the rather limited and self-interested vision of the narrator Jim Burden. Hilfer locates the true vitality of the novel in Cather's portrayal of Black Hawk, which amounts to something of a composite character existing in opposition to Jim and the "hired girls." Black Hawk's narrow, self-satisfied, yet ultimately sterile and self-denying conformity serves as a character foil, which in turn illuminates the vitality of immigrant culture. Besides his study of the small town in American fiction, from which this piece is taken, Anthony Channell Hilfer has also written *American Fiction Since 1940* (1992), and *The Crime Novel: A Deviant Genre* (1990).

Throughout Miss Cather's writings it is difficult to share her emotions regarding the Nebraska landscape and immigrant pioneer women. Miss Cather's panegyrics call too frequently for a stock response; those who have never lived in Nebraska or who do not feel a surge of conventional piety at the thought of "pioneer" may have difficulty maintaining interest in Miss Cather's novels. The problem is not merely that Miss Cather writes of things outside our experience. Mississippi is a state (and a state of mind) outside most people's experience, yet [novelist William] Faulkner's scenes and characters remain indelibly printed on the memory. Faulkner *creates* our interest in his scenes and characters whereas Willa Cather is somewhat dependent on our prior sympathy.

Her failure is one of expression. Her stories are built around intense emotions toward objects or people that are not shown to justify such emotions. In more technical terms, the objective correlatives to her emotion are inadequate. We are apparently supposed to value Thea, Alexandra, and the big red rock because Miss Cather does—this is not a good reason.[1] To be sure, her characters are supposed to embody certain values—creativity, strength, etc. But they do so in too simplified terms; they do not convince—although their enemies, the sterile conformists, are often thoroughly convincing. Worst of all, they never achieve autonomy; they are mere functions of Miss Cather. The psychological critic might object that the greatest of novelists create characters who are in some degree projections of the author's fragmented psyche; Proust is not only his narrator, Marcel, but also [his characters] Swann and the Baron de Charlus. Such a comparison only serves to clarify Miss Cather's failure. For although Proust's people have a common origin in his creative psyche, they emerge as distinctly individual characters. They may reflect Proust, but they never seem limited to this reflection; they give the illusion of living and acting in their own right, but Willa Cather's characters are limited to acting as either the mouthpieces or receivers of her emotion.

This is particularly evident in *My Ántonia* (1918). Even Miss Cather's admirers feel distressed over her narrator, Jim Burden. Jim rebels against the White Anglo-Saxon Protestant culture and the genteel dullness of Black Hawk, Nebraska, but for a young man, his rebellion is extremely mild; he merely goes to dances in order to be near the vitality of the immigrant country girls. Although he condemns the town boys for their lack of virility in allowing the desire for respectability to triumph over their sexual desires for the immigrant girls, Jim's own interest in the immigrant girls seems academic. They represent something to him rather than sexually arouse him. He does later have an affair with Lena Lingard which is notable mainly for its tepidness. The trouble is that Jim Burden is not real. Cather does not set up a fully imagined character and let him tell the story, but rather she sets up a ventriloquist's dummy and tells the story

1. Thea Kronborg and Alexandra Bergson are characters from *The Song of the Lark* and *O Pioneers!*, respectively. The "big red rock" refers to a pivotal scene from *The Song of the Lark.*

through it. If the reader realizes Jim Burden is only a device and accepts Willa Cather as the real narrator, the language and sentiments seem less stilted.

CATHER FAILED IN PORTRAYING ÁNTONIA'S FULL HUMANITY

[Cather biographer] E.K. Brown suggests that "what is excellent in *My Ántonia* does not depend on a masculine narrator. It inheres in the material itself and in appreciation of it, which might have been just as sensitive, just as various, if Willa Cather had presented her story omnisciently." Willa Cather, however, needed a narrator precisely because the excellencies of *My Ántonia* do not inhere in the material itself. Ántonia, the focus of the novel's values, is not unbelievable but neither is she very interesting. Her characterization never justifies the emotional weight Cather brings to bear upon her. Thus someone must be in the book to tell the reader how important Ántonia is; the evaluator must be a character so the reader can at least believe that the *character* feels the emotion although the reader himself is unable to. Jim Burden accounts for the presence of the emotion in the book although he cannot transfer it. The very title of the novel shows the necessity of Jim Burden. *His* Ántonia.

BLACK HAWK IS *MY ÁNTONIA'S* MOST VITAL CHARACTER

Ántonia does not justify the weight of emotion Miss Cather puts upon her, but she and the other immigrant girls in their vitality and freedom do serve as an effective foil to the narrowness and sterility of the self-complacent Anglo-Saxon citizens of Black Hawk, Nebraska. The real energy of Miss Cather's novel is in her rejection of the official culture of the town. True, the town is no [Huckleberry Finn's] Bricksville, Arkansas, but rather "a clean well-planted little prairie town." There is a curious social situation in this town. The young men of the town are all attracted to the immigrant girls who come into town to work as maids, working to help their fathers out of debt and to send the younger children in the family to school.

> Those girls had grown up in the first bitter-hard times, and had got little schooling themselves. But the younger brothers and sisters, for whom they made such sacrifices and who have had advantages, never seem to me, when I meet them now, half as interesting or as well educated. The girls, who helped to break up the wild sod, learned so much from life, from poverty, from their mothers and grandmothers; they

had all, like Ántonia, been early awakened and made obser-
vant by coming at a tender age from an old country to a new.

The immigrant girls are interesting for two reasons: they
make a fresh individual response to their new country, and
they retain vestiges of old world culture. In their individual
response to the new world, they come closer to having an or-
ganic relation to it than the older, more conventionalized
English settlers. Their freedom is compared with the narrowness and lack of vigor of the town girls:

> Physically they were almost a race apart, and out-of-door
> work had given them a vigor which, when they got over their
> first shyness on coming to town, developed into a positive
> carriage and freedom of movement, and made them conspic-
> uous among Black Hawk women.

> That was before the day of High-School athletics. . . . There
> was not a tennis-court in the town; physical exercise was
> thought rather inelegant for the daughters of well-to-do fam-
> ilies. Some of the High-School girls were jolly and pretty, but
> they stayed indoors in winter because of the cold, and in sum-
> mer because of the heat. When one danced with them, their
> bodies never moved inside their clothes; their muscles
> seemed to ask but one thing—not to be disturbed. . . .

> The daughters of Black Hawk merchants had a confident, un-
> inquiring, belief that they were "refined," and that the coun-
> try girls, who "worked out," were not.

THE NARROW SUPERIORITY OF THE TOWNSPEOPLE

The townspeople feel innately superior to the immigrants
through mere pride of race: "If I told my schoolmates that Lena
Lingard's grandfather was a clergyman, and much respected in
Norway, they looked at me blankly. What did it matter? All foreigners were ignorant people who couldn't speak English.
There was not a man in Black Hawk, who had the intelligence
or cultivation, much less the personal distinction, of Ántonia's
father. Yet people saw no difference between her and the three
Marys; they were all Bohemians, all 'hired girls'." It is this feeling of superiority that prevents intermarriage between the immigrants and the English-speaking people:

> The Black Hawk boys looked forward to marrying Black
> Hawk girls, and living in a brand-new little house with best
> chairs that must not be sat upon, and hand-painted china that
> must not be used. But sometimes a young fellow would look
> up from his ledger, or out through the grating of his father's
> bank, and let his eyes follow Lena Lingard, as she passed the
> window with her slow, undulating walk. . . .

The country girls were considered a menace to the social order. Their beauty shone out too boldly against a conventional background. But anxious mothers need have felt no alarm. They mistook the mettle of their sons. The respect for respectability was stronger than any desire in Black Hawk youth.

WICK CUTTER AND THE EVIL OF A MONEYED CULTURE

The obsessive greed and lust of Black Hawk resident Wick Cutter represent a corruption of the honest self-sacrifice and striving of immigrant farmers as they endeavor to wrest a living from the land.

It's the ogre-like Wick Cutter (the ugly name sounding both brutal and sexual) who makes the two most startling irruptions into Jim's Arcadia. 'The Hired Girls' does not end, as might have been expected, with the transcendent vision of the plough on the horizon, but with the grotesque story of the money-lender's attempt to rape Ántonia. Cutter is a vividly horrid small-town character, a gambler and lecher masquerading as a good clean-living American (he is always quoting 'Poor Richard's Almanack' and talking about the 'good old times'). His vicious treatment of his wife, whom he loves to make jealous, and whose frenzied reactions excite him more than the sex itself, is horrifyingly convincing. Ántonia goes to work for the Cutters in rebellion against Mr Harling's strictures on her dance-hall evenings, but comes back in a fright when Cutter tells her he is off on a journey, hides all his valuables under her bed, puts a heavy Yale lock on the door, and orders her to stay alone in the house. Jim takes her place for the night, and Cutter, having tricked his wife onto the wrong train, creeps back, thinking to find Ántonia, and assaults him. The scene makes an extremely disconcerting conclusion to Jim's childhood memories; why has Cather placed it there?

It is partly that Wick Cutter, like his Yale lock, is the future. . . . He stands for the debased American currency which Cather saw buying out the pioneers' values. Benjamin Franklin's 'Poor Richard's Almanack' is all about thrift; Cutter's attempted assault on Ántonia is like a miser's theft. He tries to make her as debased as the usurer's notes under the bed. The golden figure of the plough against the sun was like a glorious stamp on a coin; Cutter's licentious hoarding, by immediate contrast, introduces another system of valuation. . . . When Cutter finally murders his wife so that she won't get his property, and then kills himself, the 'spiteful' suicide is set, at the end of the book, against Mr Shimerda's at the beginning, that of a man who had nothing, and died of a broken heart.

Hermione Lee, *Willa Cather: Double Lives.* New York: Pantheon, 1989, pp. 151–52.

Later the vigorous dancing of the Bohemian girls at the Firemen's Hall is compared with the utter deadliness of the typical town life, a deadliness Willa Cather sums up in a descriptive passage:

> On starlight nights I used to pace up and down those long cold streets, scowling at the little, sleeping houses on either side, with their storm windows and covered back porches.... The life that went on in them seemed to me made up of evasions and negations; shifts to save cooking, to save washing, and cleaning, devices to propitiate the tongue of gossip. This guarded mode of existence was like living under a tyranny. People's speech, their voices, their very glances, became repressed. Every individual taste, every natural appetite, was bridled by caution. The people asleep in those houses, I thought, tried to live like the mice in their own kitchens; to make no noise, to leave no trace, to slip over the surface of things in the dark. The growing piles of ashes and cinders in the backyards were the only evidence that the wasteful, consuming process of life went on at all.

IMMIGRANT VIGOR AND NATIVE CONFORMITY

It is this kind of life that is the background for Ántonia's spontaneity. The contrast of immigrant vigor with native sterility and conformity is a trick that Willa Cather uses as well as [social critic] H.L. Mencken. She had a great deal of feeling for the immigrants, desiring to celebrate those who had conquered and to mourn those who had been broken in the new world. The village rebels were apt to look kindly on almost any variation from the native American type of middleclass Protestant English or Scotch-Irish ancestry. Thus in *Spoon River Anthology,* Masters, no Catholic, praised the Catholic priest in Spoon River, speaking in *propria persona* [his own voice] rather than through an epitaph. In Willa Cather's novels, immigrants always are more in touch with both life and art than the native born. In *The Song of the Lark,* Miss Cather had concentrated on the immigrant's spontaneous response to art; in *My Ántonia,* she concentrated on the immigrant's spontaneous response to life.

The American Dream Shapes *My Ántonia*'s Characters

Sally Peltier Harvey

My Ántonia is peopled by a vast and rich array of characters, and one significant feature they share is their respective desire for and attainment of a fair measure of "success." However, Sally Peltier Harvey argues that, in the course of the novel, the meaning of success is difficult to define. Characters such as Jim and Tiny Soderball enjoy the approval of the community and material prosperity, respectively, yet Jim is consumed by restlessness and Tiny seems no longer interested in life. Wick Cutter is a powerful and wealthy member of the Black Hawk community, but he is morally corrupt and dies a tormented man. By the standards of her time, Ántonia and her husband, Anton Cuzak, are not successful, yet there is no doubt that they have achieved a deep sense of contentment that eludes many other characters in the novel. In this manner, Cather questions and redefines success and the traditional means by which representatives of the fabled "American Dream" can and should be measured. A Ph.D. graduate from the University of California at Davis, Sally Peltier Harvey's *Redefining the American Dream* is one of the major contributions to Cather studies to appear in the last decade.

In *My Ántonia*, Ántonia Shimerda is involved in an intense project of self-development; she is shaped by the positive as well as negative pull of family, her Bohemian traditions, and the community of Black Hawk. In this respect, Ántonia is not unlike Alexandra Bergson and Thea Kronborg.[1] But in one respect, *My Ántonia* differs markedly from these earlier

1. Female characters from *O Pioneers!* (1913) and *The Song of the Lark* (1915), respectively

Excerpted from Sally Peltier Harvey, *Redefining the American Dream: The Novels of Willa Cather*. Reprinted with permission from Associated University Presses.

"success stories." Here Cather seems far more cautious about associating material success with self-fulfillment. Ántonia is Cather's first protagonist who is not, by the standards of her era, a material success. When Ántonia's childhood friend, Lena Lingard, years later talks to Jim Burden about Ántonia, Lena laments that Ántonia had not "done very well." Ántonia does not achieve fame or fortune, and only briefly leaves her little corner of Nebraska to experience—negatively—the larger world. But as a Bohemian immigrant who comes to Nebraska at the age of fourteen, she brings the traditions and values of her native country to her new corner of the world, and in the end, Ántonia achieves a happy balance between what Cather sees as "American" and "Old World" values. Ántonia shapes a new American Dream that does not rely on material success yet celebrates the wealth of opportunity in America for each individual to achieve personal goals.

In the final lines of the novel, narrator Jim Burden reflects on "those early accidents of fortune which predetermined for us [Ántonia and himself] all that we can ever be." But Jim, certainly not a reliable narrator in his appraisals of Ántonia, fails here to understand that Ántonia's life has been a journey of self-discovery, not a predetermined course. Undoubtedly, Ántonia's situation restricts her options: she is a poor immigrant and a woman in a world of narrowly defined roles for women. But throughout the novel, she still "tries on" various selves, and makes choices that extend her limits. She establishes more control over her own destiny than one might think possible in turn-of-the-century Nebraska. Ántonia is a realist. Even as a young girl, she faces the uncertainties of her future with her eyes open. She tells Jim: "Things will be easy for you. But they will be hard for us." Despite the difficulties that Ántonia faces, when we view her at the end of the novel, she apparently has found what she needs for fulfillment.

Throughout the novel, Ántonia defines her needs, responds to opportunities, and decides how to use to her advantage the situations into which "accidents of fortune" cast her. When Widow Steavens recounts to Jim Ántonia's disastrous experience with railroad man Larry Donovan, who lured her to Denver with a promise of marriage and then abandoned her, Mrs. Steavens recalls Ántonia's initial doubts about living in Denver: "'I'm a country girl,' she said.

. . . 'I was counting on keeping chickens, and maybe a cow.' "
Ántonia's doubts display her awareness of her own needs.
When Jim makes a visit to Ántonia, now living and working
on her family's farm where she is raising her child, he finds
her still just as sure of her needs: "I'd always be miserable in
a city. I'd die of lonesomeness. I like to be where I know
every stack and tree, and where all the ground is friendly. I
want to live and die here." Ántonia defines for Jim everything that she needs for fulfillment, adding: "I know what
I've got to do. I'm going to see that my little girl has a better
chance than I ever had." The Ántonia whom Jim encounters
twenty years after that conversation has found that place
"where all the ground is friendly" and has, with her husband Anton's help, provided her children with the American
Dream of "a better chance."

ANTON CUZAK'S PERSONAL DESTINY

Jim sees Anton Cuzak as "the instrument of Ántonia's special mission," but Cuzak is also involved in a project of self-
definition. Like Ántonia, Cuzak seeks a new version of the
American Dream—one in which happiness and material
success do not necessarily go hand-in-hand. As Cuzak tells
his story, we see that he, like Ántonia, has tried on various
selves to find the one that fulfills him: a journeyman furrier
in his homeland; a city-dweller in Vienna, enjoying the night
life; a simple wage-earner in New York; an orange farmer in
Florida; and finally, a hard-working but happy Nebraska
farmer. Cuzak's story is a testimonial to the American
Dream of opportunity for all. Sharing a common set of Old
World traditions, he and Ántonia have weathered hard times
to make a modest American Dream come true: "We got this
place clear now. . . . She is a good wife for a poor man," he
tells Jim, unembarrassed to call himself poor, and seemingly satisfied to have given up the glamor of city life for the
simple life on a farm. "His sociability was stronger than his
acquisitive instinct," Jim notes—Cather's sad reminder that
the standard American Dream, grounded in competition and
materialism, had by 1918 degenerated to little more than an
"acquisitive instinct."

CATHER REDEFINES SUCCESS

Throughout *My Ántonia*, Cather sets up contrasts between
those characters who achieve the American Dream of mate-

rial success, and those such as Ántonia and her husband, whose sense of fulfillment relies neither on fame, fortune, nor even on the competitive drive that pushed Thea Kronborg. The characters in *My Ántonia* who have the strongest sense of self and find the deepest satisfaction are, not surprisingly, the ones whose material success seems only modest. Cather most fully explores this idea in the contrast between Ántonia and Jim Burden. In the introduction, we meet Jim Burden, a successful lawyer who lives in New York and has married well by society's standards. The narrator, who "grew up" with Jim in Black Hawk, notes that Jim's wife "is handsome, energetic, executive," a patron of the arts, a woman with "her own fortune." But Jim Burden's apparent success has left him empty, as Cather suggests by juxtaposing the description of Jim's wife to this statement: "As for Jim, disappointments have not changed him." Thus, before *My Ántonia* even begins, we see Jim Burden—much like Bartley Alexander[2]—as a success in the world's eyes, but as an unhappy vagabond of the soul, who has found no fulfillment in either his career or his personal life. Jim comes home to himself only when he experiences with Ántonia and her family a sense of belonging that success has not brought: "My mind was full of pleasant things; trips I meant to take with the Cuzak boys. . . . There were enough Cuzaks to play with for a long while yet."

Throughout the story, Ántonia's strong sense of self contrasts sharply with Jim's passivity and indecision, his inability to define self. An orphan, Jim has only a vaguely remembered past to help him define himself when the story opens, in marked contrast to the rich past that Ántonia brings with her to Nebraska and in contrast to the exciting, colorful past of the hired man, Otto Fuchs, who at first meeting "looked lively and ferocious . . . as if he had a history." When Jim arrives in Nebraska, he feels "erased, blotted out," as if he has "left even [his parents'] spirits behind" him. But erasure can provide an opportunity for a new self-definition, if one takes that opportunity. Jim never seems to do so. When Ántonia calls him a hero after he kills a huge rattlesnake, Jim is reticent to take on such an identity: "In reality it was a mock adventure; the game was fixed for me by chance."

2. A male character from Cather's first novel, *Alexander's Bridge* (1912)

Ántonia is an active participant in her destiny, shaping her own self-image as she takes on the various roles that her circumstances force upon her. "I can work like mans now. . . . I help make this land one good farm," she boasts after her father dies and she must help her brother Ambrosch plow the fields. She cheerfully assumes the role of hired hand on others' farms; later she assumes the role of hired girl in Black Hawk at the Harling house. "Not too old to learn new ways," Ántonia as a hired girl learns the refinements of household life, but she also learns more about what she needs for happiness. When Mr. Harling tries to limit her outings to local dances, Ántonia moves out, risking the dangers of a housekeeping position at the residence of the ruthless Wick Cutter rather than restrict her own freedom to socialize and to enjoy the night life of Black Hawk.

JIM'S INCOMPLETE SUCCESS

Jim is a spectator more than a participant, defining himself through others' expectations or assessments; in contrast to Ántonia, he acquiesces to his grandparents' wish that he stop going to the firemen's dances. Even at the university in Lincoln, Jim cannot make his own decisions. He leaves Lincoln for Harvard, despite his happy relationship with his old friend from Black Hawk, Lena Lingard, because his professor, Gaston Cleric, tells him: "You won't do anything here now. . . . You won't recover yourself while you are playing about with this handsome Norwegian." Both Cleric and Jim's grandfather decide that Jim will go to Harvard, and he passively agrees, telling Lena: "I'll never settle down and grind if I stay here."

Jim's recurring dream about Lena serves to highlight his continual refusal to direct his own life and to establish his own goals. In the dream he is passively "lying against" a harvested wheat shock; Lena moves toward him, carrying a curved reaping-hook, thus appearing as a goddess of the harvest. Lena does the talking in the dream and assumes the active role: "Now they are all gone, and I can kiss you as much as I like," she tells a passive Jim. Reflecting on this dream, Jim comments: "I used to wish I could have this flattering dream about Ántonia, but I never did." The irony is that, although Jim never does have such a *dream* about Ántonia, a similar scene actually takes place between Ántonia and Jim, serving to remind the reader that Jim cannot even define what or whom he wants, much less act to realize his dreams. When Jim visits Ántonia after she has returned home with her baby, the similarities between the scene and Jim's dreamscape are striking:

> The next afternoon I walked over to the Shimerdas'. Yulka . . . told me that Ántonia was shocking wheat on the southwest quarter. I went down across the field, and Tony saw me from a long way off. She stood still by her shocks, leaning on her pitchfork, watching me as I came.

Ántonia, who is harvesting shocks of wheat as Lena was in the dream, is, like Lena, the one to speak in bold, aggressive words: "I thought you'd come, Jim. . . . I've been looking for you all day." Jim had wished that the woman who spoke invitingly to him in his recurring dream were Ántonia; but when the woman speaking invitingly to him among the harvested shocks is Ántonia, Jim remains passive and indecisive about his feelings toward her. He knows that his own sense of self is closely linked to Ántonia: "The idea of you is a part of my mind; you influence my likes and dislikes, all my tastes, hundreds of times when I don't realize it. You really are a part of me." But he cannot get any more precise than that. "I'd have liked you for a sweetheart, or a wife, or my mother or my sister," he tells Ántonia. It is safer for him to want her to be "anything that a woman can be to a man" than it is to choose a specific relationship with her. Childhood becomes his preferred refuge in this wheat-field scene: "I wished I could be a little boy again, and that my way could end there." In the last lines of the novel, we see the same retreat to the past, as Jim explains that what he shares with Ántonia is the "incommunicable past." For all the material success that Jim Burden has been able to grasp, he cannot grasp any sense of fulfillment in the present, only in a vaguely envisioned past.

THE DOUBTFUL SIDE OF THE AMERICAN DREAM

If we look at other standard success stories besides Jim's in *My Ántonia*, we see Cather continually questioning the American Dream of material success as the road to self-fulfillment. Wick Cutter is a ruthless businessman who becomes so corrupted by the drive for money that he kills his wife moments before he kills himself, making sure that he has witnesses to verify that she has died first so that her family cannot inherit his estate, which is worth, ironically, a mere one thousand dollars. Cather seems to be purposely mocking Horatio Alger's morally upright model for success by including this background on Cutter: "Cutter boasted that he never drank anything stronger than sherry, and he said he got his start in life by saving the money that other young men spent for cigars. He was full of moral maxims for boys."

Lena Lingard is not the standard model of success although she becomes a successful dressmaker in Lincoln and later in San Francisco. Jim notes that she "had none of the push and self-assertiveness that get people ahead in business." Still, Jim admires Lena's "self-possession," the trait that he lacks. Although an immigrant, Lena is Emerson's self-reliant American. She has found success and self-fulfillment although she possesses none of the standard nineteenth-century "push and self-assertiveness," nor the standard maternal or domestic instincts attributed to women. Lena chooses not to marry, preferring, she says, "to be accountable to nobody." "She remembered home as a place where there were always too many children, a cross man and work piling up around a sick woman." Her companion when Jim meets her later in San Francisco is another former "hired girl" from Black Hawk, Tiny Soderball. Jim relates Tiny's success story, remarking that "of all the girls and boys who grew up together in Black Hawk, Tiny Soderball was to lead the most adventurous life and to achieve the most solid worldly success." But although Tiny has experienced high adventure in the Klondike gold fields and has acquired great wealth through luck and hard work, she is an emotional victim of the American Dream, not its beneficiary as Lena is: "She said frankly that nothing interested her much now but making money. . . . She was satisfied with her success, but not elated. She was like someone in whom the faculty of becoming interested is worn out." Jim's remark recalls that earlier portrait of the successful Bartley Alexander as well as Cather's portrait seven years later of a successful but disillusioned Professor Godfrey St. Peter.[3]

Pianist Blind d'Arnault, who visits Black Hawk, represents another version of the American Dream. As Cather does with other minor characters, she gives us here the whole story of Blind d'Arnault's encounters with opportunity and hardship. A black man born in "the Far South . . . where the

3. The main male character in Cather's 1925 novel, *The Professor's House*

spirit if not the fact of slavery persisted," Samson d'Arnault was left blind by an illness during infancy. As a young child, d'Arnault became aware of what he needed for fulfillment when he heard the house-mistress practicing the piano. After that, nothing could keep him from his desires. One day, at the age of six, he sneaked into the parlor and approached the piano, "as if he knew it was to piece him out and make a whole creature of him." Through his desire and talent, Blind d'Arnault asserts his individuality and makes a career for himself.

Other cameo appearances in the novel highlight various versions of the American Dream: the Danish laundry girls who "were not so ambitious as Tony or Lena [but were] kind, simple girls and they were always happy"; Mrs. Gardener, who owned Black Hawk's hotel and opera house, but "seemed indifferent to her possessions"; the successful grain merchant and cattle buyer, Mr. Harling, a second-generation immigrant with a large, happy family; his daughter, Frances, who "was her father's chief clerk and virtually managed [her father's] Black Hawk office during his frequent absences," sharing that prestigious managerial position with her husband after she marries; the loyal hired hands Jake and Otto who "were the sort of men who never get on somehow," but who continued to seek their dream, going West together to work in the Yankee Girl Mine once the Burdens had moved to town; the Italians, Mr. and Mrs. Vanni, who take their "dance school" from town to town; even the unscrupulous Larry Donovan, who, after getting fired from his railroad job for "knocking down fares," goes to Mexico where "conductors get rich . . . collecting half-fares off the natives and robbing the company."

THE END OF AN ERA

Opportunities for material success abound in the world of *My Ántonia*, as Cather's portraits make clear. But some opportunities are already diminishing. When Jim, Ántonia, Lena, and Tiny picnic together at the river before Jim leaves for Lincoln, they see against the setting sun the image of a plow: "There it was, heroic in size, a picture writing on the sun." But the plow quickly diminishes from its "heroic" size as the sun sets: "That forgotten plough had sunk back to its own littleness somewhere on the prairie." Cather suggests in this image the rapidly disappearing opportunities that a vast frontier had provided. The sturdy pioneer who could carve a dream for himself with a plow and a determined will was already becoming a figure of the distant past, just as the "magnified" image of the plow against the sun so quickly faded to littleness before Jim's eyes. Cather saw in that pioneering era, as she notes in her Nebraska essay, the equation of material success with moral victory; but in the world that surrounded Cather as she wrote *My Ántonia* in 1916 and 1917, material success seemed too often an obstacle to either moral victory or self-fulfillment, as Cather's portrait of Jim Burden suggests.

THE NEED FOR COMMUNITY

Jim Burden, the most detailed portrait of the unfulfilled though successful individual in *My Ántonia*, does finally achieve a belated self-fulfillment among the Cuzaks. Thus Cather focuses in the final scenes, as she had in *The Song of the Lark*, on the importance of attachment to a community. The pull of community remains a subtext throughout *My Ántonia*. Ántonia is a loyal family member who supports the actions of her rough brother and her grasping mother. Jim, in fact, comments that "one result of [immigrants'] family solidarity was that the foreign farmers in our county were the first to become prosperous." As a hired girl in Black Hawk, Ántonia and the other hired girls form their own tight-knit community, sometimes at odds with the closed-minded citizens of Black Hawk, who, not unlike the shallow, judgmental citizens of Moonstone in *The Song of the Lark*, view the independent, energetic "country girls . . . [as] a menace to the social order." Jim Burden, walking the streets of Black Hawk late at night, reflects that in the little, flimsy houses, where people "lived like mice," life was "made up of evasions and negations." He views the community of Black Hawk as a negative counterpart to the lively, supportive community that the hired girls form.

Although Black Hawk is in many respects a negatively portrayed community, Cather emphasizes in her other portrayals of the individual's relationship to community both the obligations and the rewards of community membership. The tale of the Russian immigrants, Pavel and Peter, provides a striking example of this. As members of a wedding party in Russia, entrusted with the responsibility of driving the groom's sled through the snow-covered forest, Pavel and

Peter panic when a pack of wolves overtakes one-by-one the other sleds in the party. Desperate to make it safely to their village before the advancing wolves attack the exhausted horses, Pavel throws both bride and groom over the side of the sled to lighten the load. After this barbarous act against their community, the two are, of course, banished. The Bohemian, Krajiek, serves as another example of a person's refusal to act as a responsible member of a community. Krajiek deals unethically with the Shimerdas, his own fellow countrymen, when he sells his farm to them. In contrast to Krajiek is Anton Jelenik, a fellow Bohemian who comes to the aid of the Shimerdas when Mr. Shimerda commits suicide. "He came to us like a miracle in the midst of that grim business," Jim recalls.

Mr. Shimerda's funeral presents a positive picture of a community facing tragedy. The neighboring farmers gather for the funeral, despite the harsh winter weather, displaying a strong sense of community support that continues long after Mr. Shimerda's death, as Cather makes clear in the account of Shimerda's "grave at the crossroads." The superstitious Mrs. Shimerda insists that the grave be located there so that wagons will drive over it. But Jim points out that years afterward, when the roads were built, "the road from the north curved a little to the east just there, and the road from the west swung out a little to the south." Jim's remark stresses the sense of shared humanity and community membership that extends even to a dead foreigner, Mr. Shimerda: "I loved the spirit that could not carry out the sentence—the error from the surveyed lines, the clemency of the soft earth roads. . . . Never a tired driver passed the wooden cross, I am sure, without wishing well to the sleeper."

ÁNTONIA'S WIDER COMMUNITY

Ántonia retains a sense of community, too, about Bohemia. "I ain't never forgot my own country," she tells Jim. When he visits Ántonia's farm years later, her cultural ties are stronger than ever. She and her family speak Bohemian at home; the hollyhocks add a Bohemian touch to the farm ("the Bohemians, I remembered, always planted hollyhocks"), as the *kolaches* do to the dinner table. "Americans don't have those," one of the boys boasts of the spiced plums that they have preserved, and another remarks in Bohemian that their American visitor probably does not even know what *kolaches* are. Ántonia's son, Leo, plays Bohemian airs on his grandfather's violin; pictures from the Old Country hang on the Cuzaks' parlor walls. But the American community that so shaped Ántonia's early years in Nebraska also holds an important place among the traditions that she has passed on to her children: "These children know all about you and Charley and Sally, like as if they'd grown up with you," she tells Jim. Ántonia has thus created her own community through a healthy balance of old and new.

Cather's heroine in *My Ántonia* does not need wealth to fulfill her American Dream but, ironically, she still sees wealth as part of the dream for her children: "They have a Ford car now," she boasts of her eldest daughter, Martha, and her husband. "He's a handsome boy, and he'll be rich some day." But Ántonia seems to realize, too, that such a drive for success has its dark side: "Her husband's crazy about his farm and about having everything just right, and they almost never get away except on Sundays." Success for Ántonia means having provided her children with "a better chance." "I'm thankful none of my daughters will ever have to work out," she adds. And of her Bohemian friend, Mary, she says: "Her children will have a grand chance."

Alexander's Bridge ends with a picture of the American Dream in ruins. Pursued by a dream of self-fulfillment that he cannot clarify and thus cannot attain, [the novel's main character] Bartley Alexander is at last "released" to an almost merciful death. But Cather does not simply walk away from those ruins, nor does she become trapped in them. Instead, she salvages from the ruined dream the tools to reshape it: the acknowledgement of limits that makes self-definition possible; the drive to define one's own needs and goals; the support that a caring community offers. [Critic] John Cawelti observes that for many novelists of this era,

> the traditional ideal of success meant despair and disillusion with America, and to an extent, with human society itself. . . . The pursuit of success [became] an all-encompassing end which further separate[d] the individual from his initial goals.

Cather in these early novels moves past such "despair and disillusion" by focusing on heroines who creatively shape and courageously realize their own unique dreams.

Willa Cather's Impressionist Portraits of Ántonia and Lena

Edward J. Piacentino

Throughout her adult life, Willa Cather was a passionate follower of art and opera, and her knowledge and appreciation of the French Impressionists had a profound influence on her writing. Cather called on young writers to moderate their commitment to a kind of "photographic" realism in favor of interpreting characters and events in a more subjective manner, much as French Impressionists Monet, Renoir, and Pisarro had done in their revolutionary paintings. For Edward J. Piacentino, Ántonia and Lena Lingard offer excellent examples of Cather's impressionistic portrayal of character. Ántonia and Lena's attachment to the land allows Cather to describe these two women in supremely poetic terms. A graduate of the University of North Carolina at Chapel Hill, Edward J. Piacentino has for many years taught English at High Point University, in North Carolina.

My Ántonia, although not a work within the elitist domain of *avant garde* fiction of the early twentieth century, has generally been acclaimed Willa Cather's masterpiece. Regarded as a classic of modern American fiction, a novel with an irresistibly enduring appeal, the durability of *My Ántonia* can in part be attributed to the fact that it demonstrates the impressive quality of Cather's artistic sensibility. At different points in her career, Cather made pronouncements supporting her conviction in the high artistic potential the novel form afforded. In one of

Excerpted from Edward J. Piacentino, "A Study in Contrasts: Impressionistic Perspectives of Ántonia and Lena Lingard in Cather's *My Ántonia*," *Studies in the Humanities*, vol. 12, no. 1, June 1985. Reprinted with permission from Indiana University of Pennsylvania.

her more well-known critical dicta in "The Novel Démeublé," she remarked, "Out of the teeming, gleaming stream of the present it [the novel] must select the eternal material of art." Moreover, she hoped some of the younger writers of her time would "attempt to break away from mere verisimilitude, and following the development of modern painting, to interpret imaginatively the material and social investiture of their characters; to present their scene by suggestion rather than enumeration." This particular dimension of Cather's artistry—the use of the impressionistic method as a key strategy for character portrayal in *My Ántonia*—has been given only general critical treatment. Dorothy Tuck McFarland, for example, has generally asserted that Cather's artistry "lies primarily in her power to create with words vivid pictorial images that are imbued with an ineffable quality of felt reality." E.K. Brown, in one of the first critical assessments of the evocative quality of her descriptive method in *My Ántonia*, has noted that "everything in the book is there to convey a feeling, not to tell a story, not to establish a social philosophy, not even to animate a group of characters. The feeling attaches to persons, places, moments." A key element of the working strategy of *My Ántonia* involves the careful selection of details for the purpose of evoking suggestive feeling.

EVOKING EMOTION THROUGH IMAGERY

Because Willa Cather advocated that the transference of feeling was of the utmost importance in a novel, she seems to have consciously adopted a stylistic strategy in *My Ántonia* that closely approximates the basic method of the lyric poet: the evocation of emotion through concrete imagery; however, in carrying out her intention, she turned over the narrative responsibility to Jim Burden, who, in becoming the first-person retrospective narrator of *My Ántonia*—the controlling conscience through which the events are filtered—also functions as Cather's author-surrogate. From the information revealed in the Introduction to *My Ántonia*, we recognize Jim is not a writer by profession; rather he is a lawyer employed by one of the great western railways and thus a writer by avocation only. As many of the novel's commentators have observed, Jim is a romantic, an incurable idealist, a middle-aged malcontent, who, although dissatisfied with the state of his own present life, is still a character with an astute poetic sensibility.

THROWING OUT THE FURNITURE

In her 1922 essay "The Novel Démeublé," Willa Cather puts forward a theory that realist fiction is often "over-furnished" with unnecessary details. For Cather, greater emphasis was needed in portraying characters and events in a more subjective manner, which would in turn more faithfully record the "emotional aura of the fact or the thing or the deed."

The novel, for a long while, has been over-furnished. The property-man has been so busy on its pages, the importance of material objects and their vivid presentation have been so stressed, that we take it for granted whoever can observe, and can write the English language, can write a novel. Often the latter qualification is considered unnecessary. . . .

If the novel is a form of imaginative art, it cannot be at the same time a vivid and brilliant form of journalism. Out of the teeming, gleaming stream of the present it must select the eternal material of art. There are hopeful signs that some of the younger writers are trying to break away from mere verisimilitude, and, following the development of modern painting, to interpret imaginatively the material and social investiture of their characters; to present their scene by suggestion rather than by enumeration. The higher processes of art are all processes of simplification. The novelist must learn to write, and then he must unlearn it; just as the modern painter learns to draw, and then learns when utterly to disregard his accomplishment, when to subordinate it to a higher and truer effect. In this direction only, it seems to me, can the novel develop into anything more varied and perfect than all the many novels that have gone before. . . .

Whatever is felt upon the page without being specifically named there—that, one might say, is created. It is the inexplicable presence of the thing not named, of the overtone divined by the ear but not heard by it, the verbal mood, the emotional aura of the fact or the thing or the deed, that gives high quality to the novel or the drama, as well as to poetry itself. . . .

How wonderful it would be if we could throw all the furniture out of the window; and along with it, all the meaningless reiterations concerning physical sensations, all the tiresome old patterns, and leave the room as bare as the stage of a Greek theatre, or as that house into which the glory of Pentacost descended; leave the scene bare for the play of emotions, great and little—for the nursery tale, no less than the tragedy, is killed by tasteless amplitude. The elder Dumas enunciated a great principle when he said that to make a drama, a man needed one passion, and four walls.

Willa Cather, "The Novel Démeublé" in *Willa Cather: Stories, Poems, and Other Writings*, ed. Sharon O'Brien. New York: Library of America, 1992, pp. 834–37.

As Cather's surrogate-author, then, Jim often describes Ántonia and some of the other foreign immigrants who settle the Nebraska Divide impressionistically, sometimes almost poetically, rather than resorting to the techniques of photographic or representational realism. In his portrait of Ántonia, particularly, and to a lesser extent that of Lena Lingard, one of the Norwegian hired girls, Jim presents a series of vivid details, mainly in the form of contrasting impressionistic natural images, to accentuate some of their dominant attributes and defining personality traits and to convey his own personal impressions of and attitudes toward both characters—a practice which importantly influences how the reader ultimately perceives them.

RENDERING ÁNTONIA

Ántonia—Jim's beloved embodiment of the agrarian ideal—is mainly depicted in terms of natural, land-related images. In his initial description of Ántonia, he perceives her eyes figuratively, within an idyllic frame of reference, as "big and warm and full of light, like the sun shining on brown pools in the wood." "Her skin," Jim continues, "was brown, too, and in her cheeks she had a glow of rich, dark colour. Her brown hair was curly and wild-looking." The qualities of warmth and light seem to connote the very vitality, the evident vigor, so frequently associated with Ántonia's character throughout the novel, and anticipate the ingredients essential to the earth-goddess image Ántonia projects of herself in the last section of the book. The color brown that dominates the above passage clearly has affinities with the land itself, bringing to mind the rich hue of the fertile soil, thus serving to reinforce Ántonia's relationship to the land.

In addition, several recurring references to Ántonia's brown skin re-emphasize her close kinship to the land. In one such reference accenting Ántonia's vital nature, Frances Harling, using a metaphor drawn from a product of the land itself, tells Grandmother Burden, "She had such fine brown legs and arms, and splendid colour in her cheeks like those big dark red plums." And in the first of several reunion scenes between Jim and Ántonia, when she is twenty-four years old and back on the family farm with a child born out of wedlock, Jim avidly recalls, "I took her hands and held them against my breast, feeling once more how strong and warm and good they were, those brown hands, and remembering how many kind things they had done for me." And finally when Jim returns to the Divide and confronts Ántonia after a twenty-year absence, though she is a middle-aged veteran of an arduous life and the matron of a large family and a fertile and productive farm, he regards her affectionately, using apt images to create the desired impression: "Ántonia came in and stood before me; a stalwart, brown woman, flat-chested, her curly brown hair a little grizzled." Even though physical change is evident to Jim as he views her in this scene, still to him ". . . Ántonia had not lost the fire of life. Her skin, so brown and hardened, had not that look of flabbiness as if the sap beneath it had been secretly drawn away." In every instance cited, the vital dark brown hue of Ántonia's skin remains paramount and uniform, an emblem of the qualities of endurance and fecundity reflected in the land itself, the same land to which she has cast her destiny. In short, the recurring color imagery implicitly establishes the strong link between Ántonia and the land and thus highlights the endearing naturalness and durability of her character— qualities Jim Burden quite obviously seems to admire.

Ántonia's "curly," "wild-looking" hair can by association also be shown to share affinities to the land, particularly its features of spontaneity and freedom, unwieldly, primitive attributes, Jim often applies to the land in his descriptions of it. Typically he views such attributes positively, almost always idealistically. In Book II, the Black Hawk section, he reemphasizes this attitude in pointing out the strong bond between Ántonia and Mrs. Harling, the affable, cultured Norwegian lady for whose family Ántonia temporarily works and with whom she shares so many similarities: "They had strong, independent natures, both of them. They knew what they liked, and were not always trying to imitate other people. They loved children and animals and music, and rough play and digging in the earth. . . . Deep down in each of them there was a kind of hearty joviality, a relish of life, not over-delicate, but very invigorating."

This invigorating quality of Ántonia's personality—in part suggested by her eyes, described in terms of fire imagery as "fairly blazing with things she could not say"—becomes quite apparent in the first section of the novel when Jim relates her manner of arousing her father from one of his frequent states of depression: "Tony ran up to him, caught his hand and pressed it against her cheek. She was the only one of his family who could rouse the old man from the torpor in which he seemed to live."

Another facet of Ántonia's personality Jim admires is her stability and fortitude, a trait more distinctively masculine than feminine in Cather's treatment of it. Conveyed through natural image patterns, such traits become pragmatic for Ántonia to adopt in the spring following her father's suicide, a period during which she turns out to be the force that sustains her family. "Her neck," Jim remarks, "came up strongly out of her shoulders, like a bole of a tree out of the turf."

Book V, the final section of *My Ántonia*, represents the culmination of Jim Burden's impressionistic rendering of the heroine, the quintessence of Ántonia's idealization when she is elevated to a mythic perspective as an "earth goddess, mother earth, the madonna of the cornfields," to use [biographer] James Woodress's designation. The image of Ántonia as earth goddess fittingly reveals, [critic] John Randall observes, "the final fruition of both woman and land, which comes about because Ántonia is able to combine the vitality of nature with the order of civilization, both in her own life and in the life of the land." In Book V Cather veritably portrays Ántonia in her greatest glory. A mother of a large and happy family, Ántonia had become the matron of a fertile and prosperous farm, an apt emblem of her own personal dynamic vigor and triumph, a direct counterpoint to Jim's failure and unhappiness in his own life. In this section, moreover, Jim figuratively perceives Ántonia's maternal care and control of her children in terms of animal imagery, a fact suggesting that Ántonia, in her role as a mother, acts naturally, almost with an instinctive attentiveness: "She pulled them [her children] out of corners and came bringing them like a mother cat bringing in her kittens." In addition, Jim sees several of her children displaying the same exuberant vitality he has always associated with their mother. For example, he describes one of her sons, whom he meets when he approaches the Cuzak farm, as "fair-skinned and freckled, with red cheeks and a ruddy pelt as thick as lamb's wool, growing down his neck in little tufts." Jim sees another of her sons, Leo, as he runs toward his mother, as "like a little ram" as he "butted her playfully with his curly head." And finally when Ántonia's children emerge from their fully stocked fruit cave, as Jim and Ántonia patiently wait outside, Jim's impression—an image strikingly complementary with the fertility myth—is they are "a veritable explosion of life out of the dark cave into the sunlight."

Such vivid mental images of Ántonia's children and of her relationship with them may be interpreted as deliberate touches of Cather's artistry, a key factor in shaping the reader's attitude toward Ántonia and her family so that what he sees of them is, in effect, strongly determined by Jim's own impressionable sensibility.

As Jim concludes his visit at the Cuzak farm, fully cognizant of what Ántonia has become—"a battered woman, not a lovely girl"—he at the same time recognizes, "she still had that something which fires the imagination, could stop one's breath for a moment by a look or gesture." This climactic portrait of Ántonia is significant, for in lucidly reinforcing the image of her as a fertility symbol, Jim perceives and comprehends the source of her strength and tranquil adjustment to life: the harmonic relationship between Ántonia and the land. As Jim tenderly and nostalgically discloses, "She had only to stand in the orchard, to put her hand on a little crab apple and look up at the apples, to make you feel the goodness of planting and tending and harvesting at last. All the strong things came out of her body, that had been so tireless in serving generous emotions. . . . She was a rich mine of life." In referring to Ántonia as a "mine of life," Jim chooses an auspicious metaphor, for it serves as a reminder of Ántonia's association with the land at the novel's outset when she and her family lived in a dugout cave hewn from the very earth itself.

LENA'S SEXUALITY AND THE LAND

Though Jim Burden also portrays some of the other foreign immigrants through sometimes provocative impressionistic images to highlight facets of their personalities, none is idealized to the extent that Ántonia has been. Many of these characters, especially Lena Lingard, though they exhibit some of the heroine's vitality (they too spend their formative years on the Divide on family farms), they, unlike Ántonia, eventually withdraw permanently from the land, the point of origin, so Cather intimates, of vital essence.

Of the several Norwegian hired girls Cather portrays, Lena Lingard, through the imagery used to describe her, is shown to be the very antithesis of Ántonia. Cather consistently describes Lena, whom Jim affectionately admires and

with whom he falls in love briefly during his college years at
the University of Nebraska, in light color tones, the converse
of the brown tones so frequently associated with Ántonia. In
fact the name Lena derives from the Greek appelation, He-
lena, meaning torch or light one. She is described as a
"plump, fair-skinned girl . . . , demure and pretty." "Her yellow hair," Jim observes, "was burned to a ruddy thatch on
her head; but her legs and arms, curiously enough, in spite
of constant exposure to the sun, kept a miraculous whiteness. . . ." Another feature Jim stresses about Lena is her
eyes, "candid eyes, that always looked a little sleepy under
their long lashes . . . ," giving her a lethargic countenance
that contrasts to Ántonia's prominent vivacity. Moreover,
Lena is repeatedly depicted in relation to soft, gentle, delicate objects—silks, satins, fine clothes—and when Jim first
encounters her at the Harlings, he observes her keen attraction to the "cheerful rooms with naive admiration."

Yet Jim's relationship with Lena is far from Platonic; he
comes to be charmed, in a romantic sense, by her beauty, by
her unrestrained radiance, and by her delicate nature. And
while living in Black Hawk, Jim has a recurring dream
about Lena, a dream that reflects his erotic impression of
her. When he recounts this dream, he does so using a pattern of natural, light-related imagery: "I was in a harvest-
field full of shocks, and I was lying against one of them.
Lena Lingard came across the stubble barefoot, in a short
shirt, with a curved reaping-hook in her hand, and she was
flushed like the dawn, with a kind of luminous rosiness all
about her. She sat beside me, turned to me with a soft sigh
and said, 'Now they are all gone, and I can kiss you as much
as I like.'" If such gentle, fanciful imagery fails to create the
impression Jim seeks to convey convincingly and to establish the desired contrast with Ántonia, then his after-
thoughts about this dream make the point of opposition intended clear: "I used to wish I could have this flattering
dream about Ántonia, but I never did."

Later, when Jim carries on a brief romantic affair with
Lena in Lincoln, where she has set up her own dress-
making shop, he again gives his impressions of her, using
predominantly soft, natural, light imagery. In his frequent
meetings with Lena in downtown Lincoln after his morning
classes, she seemed to him "as fresh as the spring morning,"
and her gentle vigor is enhanced by the jonquils or the hy-

acinth plants she carried with her. Furthermore, he perceives the tone of her voice as "soft, with her caressing into-
nation and arch naivete." To hear Lena's voice becomes a
pleasant diversion for Jim, for she "was almost as candid as
Nature." "Lena," Jim further muses, "was never so pretty as
in the morning; she wakened fresh with the world every day,
and her eyes had a deeper colour then, like the blue flowers
that are never so blue as when they first open."

The converse of Ántonia, Lena, like Jim, leaves the land,
becoming, James Woodress points out, "a Benjamin
Franklin type who works hard, builds a business, prospers,
and remains devoutly attached to the work ethic."

Edith Lewis, a life-long friend of Willa Cather, noted in
her appreciative biography of the author that Cather felt *My
Ántonia* "was the best thing she had done—that she has succeeded, more nearly than ever before, in writing the way she
wanted to write." In adopting as one angle of her artistic
strategy the imagistic method in delineating impressionistically personality traits both of Ántonia and Lena Lingard,
Cather ably demonstrated that she could give solid sub-
stance to her precept: "that in writing novels as in poetry,
the facts are nothing, the feeling is everything," feeling effectively evoked and artfully transmitted through carefully
selected and skillfully wrought image patterns. True to her
own high standards of artistic integrity, true to her concep-
tion that the novel is an art form, Willa Cather, in the dis-
cerning judgment of Dorothy Tuck McFarland, created in
My Ántonia a novel with a "seemingly artless surface [but
which actually] is . . . the result of the most careful artistry."

CHAPTER 4

Critical Debates over *My Ántonia*

READINGS ON
MY ÁNTONIA

Ántonia Becomes a Lifeless Object Rather than a Living Character

William J. Stuckey

According to critic William J. Stuckey, in order to consecrate his past as an attractive alternative to his dissatisfied present, Jim Burden transforms Ántonia Shimerda's life into a work of art, and Ántonia herself into an art object. Correspondingly, Stuckey sees the novel as lifeless; its potentially compelling raw materials have in effect been smothered by Jim's nostalgic idealizations, and his determination to have characters from his past conform to his unrealistic vision of an agrarian paradise. Most importantly, Stuckey sees Jim Burden and Willa Cather as inseparable, and therefore equates Jim's failings as a narrator with Cather's failings as a writer. William J. Stuckey was a professor of English at Purdue University in Indiana.

Critics who are most committed to defending Willa Cather's integrity as an artist seem to have developed a talent for talking about *My Ántonia* out of both sides of their mouths. For though Miss Cather's admirers have found much to praise in the individual parts of this book, they have turned up a fairly large number of serious flaws as well. It is generally acknowledged, for example, that the book is very loosely organized, that many incidents have no apparent function in the novel, and that though it is supposed to be about Ántonia, most of the five books that make up the novel are about the narrator, Jim Burden. Even more damaging has been the critics' admission that, in spite of Jim Burden's assertion that he would have liked to have had Ántonia for a wife, there is little in the novel to support this. Indeed, one critic has said that there is an emotional emptiness in Jim and Ántonia's relationship.

Excerpted from William J. Stuckey, "*My Ántonia:* A Rose for Miss Cather," *Studies in a Novel,* vol. 4, no. 3, Fall 1972. Copyright © 1972 North Texas State University. Reprinted with permission from the publisher.

The conclusion of *My Ántonia* has also given some critics pause, for although it is this section that does most to create the beautiful symbolic Ántonia, there is the feeling among some readers that this is a tacked-on happy ending and, further, that the method of creating this beauty is not altogether honest. Instead of pursuing the implications of their insights, however—by asking how these flaws may be squared with the rest of the novel—critics have either set them aside or found a means of explaining them away. And so, the general impression one gets from reading Cather's critics is that *My Ántonia* is a beautiful book celebrating agrarian values, but that it is not one that will bear much looking into.

This attitude is hardly a compliment either to Willa Cather or to *My Ántonia*, for though it may help preserve the popular view that *My Ántonia* is an inspired novel about a vital, dynamic earth mother living on the Nebraska frontier, it keeps us from exploring the contradictions beneath the surface story. And surely, unless those contradictions are faced, we cannot say with much conviction what this novel actually is about.

One way to square these contradictions with the surface events of the story is to see that though *My Ántonia* is ostensibly about Ántonia, actually, technically, it is about what Ántonia *comes to mean* to Jim Burden.

This is not a trivial distinction, as I shall try to show, for though there is much in the novel that cannot be fully brought into a single design, much of it can be seen as a consistently playing down, even a denying of what Ántonia is, and a playing up of what Jim Burden is finally able to make her into. And so it might be said that *My Ántonia* is not so much the story of Ántonia's agrarian success, as it is Jim Burden's success in converting her into a symbol of a way of life that he approves of. This is not to say, of course, that the details of Ántonia's life are not an important part of Jim's story. They are. But they are also the raw materials from which Jim Burden is able to select those things that can be made to fit *his* picture of Ántonia. In the process, some of this raw material has to be suppressed. And it is this suppression, particularly in the conclusion, that strikes some readers as dishonest. But if one sees how this suppression follows logically from what has gone before, then it will seem no more or less dishonest than the rest of the book.

Ántonia Becomes a Symbol

The general pattern of Jim Burden's success comes from his desire to convert Ántonia into a beautiful image of agrarian life and Ántonia's resistance to that conversion—a pattern that might be sketched somewhat as follows: at first Jim is attracted to Ántonia's warmth and vitality, but at the same time repelled by the grosser aspects of her behaviour; later, while still drawn to her, he is further repelled by her growing crudeness and, still later, by the way she is attracted to other men. It is not masculine jealousy that Jim appears to feel, but some deep sense of outrage and frustration. He likes Ántonia and wants to approve of her, but her manners and her animal vitality prevent him from doing so. As a consequence, Jim's relationship with Ántonia shifts back and forth between liking and disgust.

The high point of Jim's disgust comes after a fight between Jim and Wick Cutter, a would-be seducer of Ántonia. After the fight, Jim says that he hates Ántonia and that he never wants to see her again. Shortly thereafter (and apparently without being reconciled with her), Jim goes away to the University at Lincoln. There, from reading Virgil, he comes to understand that without vital, earthy girls (like Ántonia, though he does not specifically name her) there would be no poetry. This insight appears to be a turning point in Jim's relationship with Ántonia, for when he goes home and discovers that she has been seduced by a cheap ladies' man named Larry Donovan and has borne his child, he is not shocked or disgusted. Instead, he is able to think of Ántonia in a wholly idealized way. When he goes East to Harvard Law School, he carries with him a warm and happy image of his childhood friend.

In the concluding section of the novel, Jim rounds out his beautiful portrait of Ántonia. He has returned to Nebraska after an absence of twenty years and has found in Ántonia's life nothing to shock or dismay him. Indeed, he is able to see in her and in the beautiful family and the fine orchard and fertile farm she has created a symbol for the source of civilization itself.

The pattern I have described starts at the beginning of the novel, shortly after Jim and Ántonia meet. Jim, of course, does not know Ántonia very well and is not as deeply attracted to her as he is later to become, but he "snuggles" down with her in the prairie grass and admires the beauty of the landscape. He thinks Ántonia "quick and very eager" and remarks that it was "wonderfully pleasant" there with the blue sky over them and the gold tree in front. Then Ántonia spoils the beauty of the occasion by making a gesture that Jim regards as too familiar. She offers him "a little chased silver ring she wore on her middle finger. When she coaxed and insisted" that he take it, Jim "repulsed her quite sternly." He remarks, "I didn't want her ring, and I felt there was something reckless and extravagant about her wishing to give it away to a boy she had never seen before." These are to be Ántonia's most exasperating qualities—her extravagant vitality and her improper behaviour, for the early Jim can be wholly content with her only when her vitality is checked by what he sees as appropriate formal gestures.

The same problem occurs again in the "rattlesnake incident," except that instead of being overly friendly, Ántonia is now being overly oppressive. Just previous to this incident, Ántonia has been "taking a superior tone" with Jim and he resents it. It is not that he wants Ántonia's affection. What he wants is for her to behave toward him the way a girl should behave toward a boy. The encounter with the snake, which Jim kills, terrifies Ántonia, and Jim's bravery in killing it chastens her into paying him the deference he feels is his due. "She liked me better from that time on, and she never took a supercilious air with me again. I had killed a big snake—I was now a big fellow." This incident is handled rather lightly and Jim's wish to be treated as a "big fellow" is no doubt humorously meant. Still, it is significant that Jim's dissatisfaction, here again, is due to Ántonia's refusal to take what he regards as a proper attitude toward him. And, also significant, she pleases him only when she expresses that attitude.

JIM IS AN IMAGE-MAKER

There is in the novel, as I have said, a good deal that cannot be assimilated to this pattern. Our concern, however, is with Jim the image-maker, not with Ántonia, the raw material on which the image draws. Still, the things that Jim chooses to tell about his grandparents and about their home, about the town of Black Hawk and the townspeople, and especially what he says about Ántonia's family, fall more fully into place when one sees how they are related to this pursuit of a forced image of excellence. Take, for example, the way Jim creates for us an image of his grandparents. There are a number of characters in the book that are treated with astringent realism, but the Burdens are handled as gently as if they were two valuable old woodcuts. They are homely, to be sure, for they are country people, but they are spotlessly beautiful. Their manners and dress, the way they treat Jim and the hired hands, their relations with their neighbors, the way they conduct their household—all possess a kind of aloof serenity. The Burden grandparents, it seems, have achieved a perfection of form that Jim wants Ántonia to have.

Jim's trouble lies, of course, in his initial failure to see that Ántonia will not be able to learn that form from his grandparents. But then Jim is not concerned with reasons. He merely sees how imperfect Ántonia and her family are and he displays their imperfections with harsh clarity. The Shimerdas are pictured by Jim as dirty, disorganized, inept, and ill-mannered. Whereas the Burden grandparents never exhibit any unattractive emotions, the Shimerdas appear to do nothing but quarrel, whine, steal, and beg. Only Mr. Shimerda, the Austrian violinist, keeps up an attractive exterior and significantly is the only one among the Shimerdas who deeply appreciates the Burdens' good manners. Indeed, he finds their well-ordered house a civilized refuge in an otherwise savage world. When Mr. Shimerda takes his life, Jim has the feeling that the old violinist's soul visits the Burdens' house before departing for the next world. Jim thinks that had Mr. Shimerda been able to live in the Burdens' house, "this terrible thing would never have happened."

JIM'S RESISTANCE TO ÁNTONIA'S TRUE SELF

As Jim gets to know Ántonia better, his difficulty with her reduces to the unpleasant fact that she prefers to be more like her family than like his. That is why Jim grows angry with Ántonia when she takes her family's side in a fight with one of the Burdens' hired hands, and that is why he is so repelled by her when she imitates her brother's crude table manners. It does not occur to Jim to admire Ántonia's loyalty to her family or to see that table manners are not a reliable indication of human worth. Here again, what is important to Jim is how Ántonia behaves and, at this point in the novel, he cannot accept her behaviour.

Essentially the same thing is brought out, but in a positive manner, on the one occasion in the early part of the book when Ántonia deeply pleases Jim. A number of things have happened just before this to make Jim vow he will never be friends with the Shimerdas again, but then Ántonia (unaccountably) comes to work for Jim's grandmother and now that Ántonia is under the Burdens' roof Jim is delighted with her. "We were glad to have her in the house," Jim says. "She was so gay and reponsive that one did not mind her heavy, running step, or her clattery way with pans." And Ántonia pleases Jim by expressing her liking for the Burden household. "I like your grandmother," she tells him, "and all things here." Jim comes back, "Why aren't you always nice like this, Tony?"

If Tony had remained in the Burden household or, later, had stayed in the cultivated Harling household (where she continues to be a "nice" motherly hired girl), Jim might have been able to keep her high in his estimation, but Ántonia's old wilfulness reasserts itself along with her animal vitality. She insists on going to the notorious Saturday night tent dances and this indecorous behaviour causes her to lose her position with the Harlings. Perversely, it seems to Jim, Ántonia goes to work for Wick Cutter, an infamous woman chaser. Mrs. Harling predicts that Ántonia will "have a fling" at the Cutters that she "won't get up from in a hurry." As it turns out, Ántonia does have her fling, but it is Jim who has trouble getting up. In an attempt to protect Ántonia's honor from Wick Cutter, he gets his eye blackened and his lip cut. This experience deeply depresses him. He says that he hates Ántonia for having let him in "for all of this disgustingness."

This incident perhaps more than any other one gives us an important insight into Jim's attachment to Ántonia. His interest is not the conventionally romantic one that some readers have tried to find (and which Miss Cather to some extent encourages). Jim does not love Ántonia as a man would. His feeling for her is that of a child who "hero-worships" an older person. He wants to admire and look up to Ántonia and, of course, he is inevitably disappointed. It never occurs to Jim to question his demands on Ántonia. He is too preoccupied with his ideal of her.

The solution for getting Ántonia permanently enshrined in Jim's admiration is not directly presented in the novel. Jim simply goes off to the university at Lincoln, acquires a certain distance from her, along with an insight by way of Virgil into the poetic worth of primitive women, which hardly prepares us for his ability to accept so readily behaviour from Ántonia (her "elopement" with Larry Donovan and the illegitimate baby) that would have shocked him earlier. But the problem for the skeptical reader is that Jim does not really accept what Ántonia has done. He avoids it or, more accurately, his author arranges matters so that none of the potentially unpleasant details are allowed to get through to Jim. He learns of Ántonia's affair indirectly, and through a woman who likes Ántonia very much and who therefore puts her situation in an attractive light. His only contacts with Ántonia's baby, moreover, are in a photographer's studio where he notices a picture of it ("one of those depressing 'crayon enlargements' often seen in farm-house parlours"), and, later, when given a quick look by Ántonia's sister. Then when Jim sees Ántonia again, he sees her alone, out-of-doors, under a beautiful sky and against a backdrop of trees and shocks of wheat. Ántonia almost spoils the beauty of this meeting by talking about her little girl, but Jim, who perhaps is clinging fast to his revelation from Virgil, quickly lifts the conversation to a higher plane. "Do you know, Ántonia," he says, "since I've been away, I think of you more often than of anyone else in this part of the world. I'd have liked to have you for a sweetheart, or a wife, or my mother or my sister—anything that a woman can be to a man. The idea of you is part of my mind. . . . You really are a part of me."

JIM'S IDEALIZATION OF ÁNTONIA

Jim has at last succeeded in getting Ántonia detached from the disappointing realities of her life and converted into a beautiful picture he can carry East with him when he goes off to Harvard.

It takes twenty years for the full idealization of Ántonia to take place. And during that time she has had the opportunity not only to increase in her ability to reflect Jim's ideal, but to take on the ability to reflect the timeless pattern of civilization as well. She is married now, the mother of eleven children, the mistress of a fertile farm and a well-ordered household. She can no longer spoil Jim's ideal of her, for she is, from Jim's point of view, a completed, finished person. And he is only a visitor in her house, a status that gives him the distance and detachment necessary to his idealization. Gone are both the appearance and the necessity for seeing anything unpleasant in Ántonia's life; instead are manifesta-

tions of the rural virtues that Jim associates with his grandparents and their beautifully managed old farm: cleanliness,
order, decorum. The only vestige of the Shimerda household
is, happily, the violin that once belonged to Ántonia's unhappy father, which two of Ántonia's children play, with less
than moderate success. For it is not the fine arts that Ántonia comes to symbolize for Jim Burden, but the domestic
ones. He is able to see her permanently at last, as the maker
of formal gestures which, he says, "we recognize by instinct
as universal and true."

From the standpoint of ordinary human behaviour, Jim
Burden's interest in Ántonia is unconvincing. This is implied in [biographer] E.K. Brown's suggestion that Miss
Cather might better have employed a feminine point of view.
Perhaps. But this is like saying she might better have given
us a different Ántonia. We have no way of knowing what
Ántonia might have been (or, indeed, whether she would
have been) had Cather chosen to create her from a different
point of view. All we have is what we have been given. Nor
need we believe that Jim Burden is a real man in order to accept the fact that Cather used him to create *her* Ántonia. Jim
Burden, convincing or not, is the special consciousness out
of which Ántonia has been brought before us and we cannot
separate the two.

Most writers, whether deliberately or not, try to keep the
special consciousness out of which a novel comes from
showing—perhaps because the process of writing fiction is
an evasion as well as an affirmation. In *My Ántonia* Cather
did something most unusual. She not only allowed this special consciousness to show; she put it in the forefront of her
story and, whether she meant to or not, made it the chief focus of attention. She did that, I believe, out of psychological
as well as artistic necessity. . . .

A failure of technique in a writer of Willa Cather's talent
is more than a technical failure, of course. It is a failure of
sensibility as well. For what is significant about Jim Burden
is not that he is a clumsy device the reader must somehow
see around, but that Cather chose to use him in the first
place and that she kept on using him even when it must
have been apparent that he was not working. But technique,
if I may shift the perspective somewhat, is often the result of
compromise between what the writer wishes to say and
what, given the material he has to work with and the nature

of his sensibility, he is able to write. In this sense, the point of view from which a novel is told is the writer himself, or as much of him as we can ever know.

Willa Cather, when pressed by critics who complained that *My Ántonia* was not a novel, maintained that it was not intended as such. It was, she said, simply about people she had once known. Technical failures cannot be so easily explained away. *My Ántonia*, though evidently based on the facts of Willa Cather's life, obviously is fiction. Still, it is more autobiographical than Willa Cather's other fiction, not just because it closely follows those facts (often in a pointless way) but because it reveals a side of her that does not show itself so visibly in her other novels. Jim Burden is, in an important sense, Willa Cather, and *My Ántonia* demonstrates the way Cather's imagination set about converting the raw materials of experience into art. For her, the creation of fiction was not the striking of a balance between personal feeling and the facts of experience. . . . For Cather, it was the imposing of her strong and intensely personal feelings upon a sometimes intractable world. The much admired image of the "plough against the sun," for example, illustrates specifically the way her imagination worked. The plough that Jim and the hired girls see magnified into heroic size against the setting sun can stand as a symbol for the real world; the sun, for the writer's vision which lifts up that world and intensifies it to match the writer's feelings. This imaginative process, however, is partly a romantic heightening, partly a matter of excluding what is ugly or extraneous. . . .

Willa Cather's talent for beautifying worked best when it was called upon to deal with things remote, with landscapes, village streets, houses, groups of people, or single persons detached from relationships with others and caught in a characteristic attitude. It was the surface of life and isolated moments of exalted emotion that gave Willa Cather her most satisfying clues to the meaning of experience. Jim Burden's problem with Ántonia was Willa Cather's problem as well, possibly because Ántonia was based upon someone in her own past whom she had known too personally to romanticize completely. It was only when, like Jim Burden, she had put time and distance between her and her past, after having lived long enough in Pittsburgh and, later in New York, that she could see it in the beautiful way her imagination required. . . .

The story of Jim Burden's struggle and final success with Ántonia is, then, the story of an artist who triumphs over life by converting it into an art object. This, of course, is what all artists do, but Cather has taken it a step farther; she has put the artistic process into the center of her story. A novelist like Fitzgerald or Hemingway or Henry James (to name a writer Miss Cather is said most to resemble) uses art to catch the very feel of life itself. At the end of novels like *The Great Gatsby, A Farewell to Arms,* and *The Portrait of a Lady* (a James novel that illustrates, I believe, how little of the essential James is in Willa Cather) there is a final opening out of the fictional world into the world of reality. Gatsby is delivered from his cocoon of illusion into the frighteningly real world of men. Frederic Henry walks out of romance into the cold and sobering rain, and Isabel Archer is at last made to see the ugly truth her romantic imagination had concealed from her. These conclusions, of course, are still fictions, but the intent one senses behind them is to make them resemble the world of actual experience.

The intent one senses behind the conclusion of *My Ántonia,* on the contrary, is to lift Ántonia out of her "real" world into a world of changeless art. The Ántonia of the final pages of this novel—the vital, irrepressible Ántonia—has become at last the beautiful tomb of Jim Burden's past.

A Flawed but Impressive Achievement

David Daiches

One of the major criticisms of *My Ántonia* is that the character of Ántonia Shimerda is lost amid Jim Burden's many digressions and an abundance of subplots that are only indirectly connected to her. Yet these shortcomings have never detracted from *My Ántonia*'s continuing appeal to readers. While acknowledging the novel's flaws, David Daiches maintains that its strength lies in its vivid portrayal of a number of powerful episodes. Eschewing a carefully plotted, linear development that leads to one climactic event and its resolution, the novel's effect is cumulative and impressionistic. As a result, the novel successfully assumes a unique emotional rhythm that ultimately satisfies readers. David Daiches is an emeritus professor of English at the University of Edinburgh. He has written many books of criticism, including studies of Virginia Woolf, D.H. Lawrence, and Robert Burns.

My Ántonia, which appeared in 1918, is another story of pioneering life in Nebraska. Like *O Pioneers!* it contains autobiographical elements—the heroine was suggested by "a Bohemian girl who was good to me when I was a child"—and is concerned with the conflict between memory and desire, nostalgia and ambition, in the immigrant. The European background, which lies behind the book like a fascinating mystery, is both attractive and disturbing: the picturesque and feudal Bohemia for which Mr. Shimerda languishes is but one aspect of a background which includes the horror of the Russian scene where famished wolves pursue a bridal party returning

182 Readings on My Ántonia

home during the night. Yet, for all the tensions between the Old World and the New to be found in this novel as in so many of the others, the central theme is neither the struggle of the pioneer nor the conflict between generations, but the development and self-discovery of the heroine. This suggests a structure like that of *The Song of the Lark;* but in fact the book is organized much more like *O Pioneers!* We do not follow the heroine's career in the anxious detail we find in the preceding novel. Although Willa Cather did not at the time agree with [publisher] Heinemann's criticism of *The Song of the Lark* and its "full-blooded method," she tells us that "when the next book, *My Ántonia,* came along, quite of itself and with no direction from me, it took the road of *O Pioneers!*—not the road of *The Song of the Lark.*"

ÁNTONIA IS A SYMBOLIC CHARACTER

The story is told in the first person by Jim Burden, childhood friend of the heroine and now "legal counsel for one of the great Western railways." This device gives proper voice to the autobiographical impulse which lies behind much of the book; but it has its dangers. No observer, however knowing and sympathetic, can tell the full story of the development of a character like Ántonia. A character who is constantly talked about, described, and discussed but who never reveals herself fully and directly to the reader tends to become the kind of symbol the observer wants to make of her, an objectification of the observer's emotions, and this in large measure does happen to Ántonia. Her growth, development, and final adjustment is a vast symbolic progress interesting less for what it is than for what it can be made to mean.

This is in some degree true also of Alexandra Bergson in *O Pioneers!,* who emerges at the end of the book as a kind of Earth Goddess symbolic of what the pioneers had achieved on the Nebraska plains. There is an epic quality in *O Pioneers!* which makes one resent the intrusion of incidents drawn to a smaller scale. That epic quality is lacking in *My Ántonia:* the cultivation of the land is not something *achieved* by Ántonia, but something in which she submerges herself in order to attain salvation. She ends as the ideal wife and mother, bound to the farming life, more devoted than ever to the open spaces: but it is not she who has made that life possible or tamed those open spaces so much as it is that life and those spaces which have saved her.

THE PROBLEM OF PERSPECTIVE

Throughout the book the narrator's sensibility takes control; and this raises problems which Willa Cather is never quite able to solve. The narrator's development goes on side by side with Ántonia's: indeed, we sometimes lose sight of Ántonia for long stretches at a time, while we can never lose sight of the narrator. Miss Cather tries to solve this problem by emphasizing that the book's title is *My Ántonia:* this is not just the story of Ántonia, but of Ántonia as she impinged on a number of other significant characters. She goes out of the way to use the adjective "my" in talking of Ántonia with reference not only to the narrator but also to other characters—to her father, who first uses the phrase, and to Mrs. Steavens, for example. And yet we cannot say that this is a story of what Ántonia meant to a selected number of other characters of the book: though there are elements in the story which suggest this, the organization as a whole tends to present Ántonia as a symbolic figure in her own right rather than as a character with special meaning for particular individuals. . . .

THE BURDENS AND THE SHIMERDAS

The relation between the Burdens and the Shimerdas is at the beginning that of relatively prosperous neighbors to a distressed immigrant family. The Shimerdas had not been fairly dealt with by the Bohemian homesteader from whom they had bought their land and sod house, and they found conditions appalling on arrival. Had it not been for the assistance of the Burdens they would not have survived their first winter in Nebraska. Jim and Ántonia are thrown together from the beginning, and from the beginning Ántonia, in spite of her fragmentary English and humbler circumstances, is the dominating character. Together they explore the countryside and learn to know and love the Nebraska plains. Incidents are contrived by the author to bring out different aspects of the Nebraska scene and atmosphere, and there is some impressive descriptive writing.

There are episodes in this first part of the book that have little if any relation to the story of Ántonia's development— the story of the two Russians, Peter and Pavel, for example. Mr. Shimerda, who could understand their language, made friends with them, but soon afterward Pavel died, and on his deathbed he told the terrible story of how as a young man in

Russia he had thrown a bride and groom off a sledge to the pursuing wolves in order to save himself from certain death. This is a remarkable little inset story, but its relation to the novel as a whole is somewhat uncertain. It was soon after the death of Pavel and the subsequent departure of Peter that Mr. Shimerda committed suicide. By this time it was midwinter, and the atmosphere of the frozen landscape is effectively employed to emphasize the pity and horror of this death from homesickness.

Mr. Shimerda had hoped to see Ántonia get a good American education, but after his death she took her place as one of the workers on the farm, to which she devoted all her time. . . .

For all her devotion to her father's memory, Mr. Shimerda's mantle does not fall on Ántonia, but rather on Jim, who responds to the suggestion of a rich European culture lying behind his melancholy. This is the first of a series of influences that lead him eventually to the university and a professional career in the East, yet in a profound if indirect way it draws him closer to Ántonia. . . .

The first section of *My Ántonia* ends with a brilliant summer scene. Ántonia and Jim watch an electric storm from the slanting roof of the Burdens' chicken house:

> The thunder was loud and metallic, like the rattle of sheet iron, and the lightning broke in great zigzags across the heavens, making everything stand out and come close to us for a moment. Half the sky was chequered with black thunderheads, but all the west was luminous and clear: in the lightning flashes it looked like deep blue water, with the sheen of moonlight on it; and the mottled part of the sky was like marble pavement, like the quay of some splendid sea-coast city, doomed to destruction. Great warm splashes of rain fell on our upturned faces. One black cloud, no bigger than a little boat, drifted out into the clear space unattended, and kept moving westward. All about us we could hear the felty beat of the raindrops on the soft dust of the farmyard. Grandmother came to the door and said it was late, and we would get wet out there.
>
> "In a minute we come," Ántonia called back to her. "I like your grandmother, and all things here," she sighed. "I wish my papa live to see this summer. I wish no winter ever come again."
>
> "It will be summer a long while yet," I reassured her. "Why aren't you always nice like this, Tony?"
>
> "How nice?"

"Why, just like this; like yourself. Why do you all the time try to be like Ambrosch?"

She put her arms under her head and lay back, looking up at the sky. "If I live here, like you, that is different. Things will be easy for you. But they will be hard for us."

THE PORTRAIT OF BLACK HAWK

After three years on the farm Jim and his grandparents move to the "clean, well-planted little prairie town" of Black Hawk. The second section of the book concerns life in Black Hawk. Ántonia has to be brought in, so Miss Cather contrives to have her engaged as a cook by the Harlings, the

---

A NOVEL THAT EVOKES THE ETERNAL TRAGEDY OF MAN

Brilliant and caustic, H.L. Mencken was one of the most influential cultural critics of the early twentieth century, and his reviews had the power to ruin or dramatically further a novelist's career. Fortunately for Willa Cather, Mencken was a lifelong admirer of her work, as this 1919 review of My Ántonia *vividly illustrates.*

Miss Cather is a craftsman whom I have often praised in this place, and with increasing joy. Her work, for ten years past, has shown a steady and rapid improvement, in both matter and manner. She has arrived at last at such a command of the mere devices of writing that the uses she makes of them are all concealed—her style has lost self-consciousness; her feeling for form has become instinctive. And she has got such a grip upon her materials—upon the people she sets before us and the background she displays behind them—that both take on an extraordinary reality. I know of no novel that makes the remote folk of the western prairies more real than *My Ántonia* makes them, and I know of none that makes them seem better worth knowing. Beneath the swathings of balderdash, the surface of numskullery and illusion, the tawdry stuff of Middle Western *Kultur,* she discovers human beings embattled against fate and the gods, and into her picture of their dull struggle she gets a spirit that is genuinely heroic, and a pathos that is genuinely moving. It is not as they see themselves that she depicts them, but as they actually are. To representation she adds something more. There is not only the story of poor peasants, flung by fortune into lonely, inhospitable wilds; there is the eternal tragedy of man.

William H. Nolte, ed., *H.L. Mencken's Smart Set Criticism.* Ithaca, NY: Cornell University Press, 1968, pp. 264–66.

family who live next door to the Burdens in their new home. It is, perhaps, a rather artificial device to move the heroine temporarily into the narrator's town in order to keep her under his eye, but the sequence of events which brings this about are not improbable in terms of the story as told. What is more dubious is the relation of this whole section of the novel to the main theme of the story. It is in itself a brilliantly written section. Life in the small prairie town is described with a cunning eye for the significant detail, and a fine emotional rhythm runs through the whole. The daughters of the immigrant (mostly Swedish) farmers in the country round about have come into town to get positions as maids and thereby help their families to improve their economic position: Jim and Tony move happily in these humble circles, whose healthy gaiety is sharply contrasted with the narrow stuffiness of the tradespeople and their families. . . .

The feeling that it is the imaginative immigrant and not the stuffy conventional American who is responsible for the country's greatness recurs again and again in Miss Cather's novels:

> The daughters of Black Hawk merchants had a confident, unenquiring belief that they were "refined," and that the country girls, who "worked out," were not. The American farmers in our country were quite as hard-pressed as their neighbours from other countries. All alike had come to Nebraska with little capital and no knowledge of the soil they must subdue. All had borrowed money on their land. But no matter in what straits the Pennsylvanian or Virginian found himself, he would not let his daughters go out into service. Unless his girls could teach a country school, they sat at home in poverty.
>
> The Bohemian and Scandinavian girls could not get positions as teachers, because they had no opportunity to learn the language. Determined to help in the struggle to clear the homestead from debt, they had no alternative but to go into service. . . . But every one of them did what she had set out to do, and sent home those hard-earned dollars. The girls I knew were always helping to pay for ploughs and reapers, brood-sows, or steers to fatten.
>
> One result of this family solidarity was that the foreign farmers in our country were the first to become prosperous. After the fathers were out of debt, the daughters married the sons of neighbours—usually of like nationality—and the girls who once worked in Black Hawk kitchens are to-day managing big farms and fine families of their own; their children are better off than the children of the town women they used to serve.
>
> I thought the attitude of the town people toward these girls very stupid. If I told my schoolmates that Lena Lingard's

grandfather was a clergyman, and much respected in Norway, they looked at me blankly. What did it matter? All foreigners were ignorant people who couldn't speak English. There was not a man in Black Hawk who had the intelligence or cultivation, much less the personal distinction, of Ántonia's father. Yet people saw no difference between her and the three Marys; they were all Bohemians, all "hired girls."

I always knew I should live long enough to see my country girls come into their own, and I have. . . .

A passage such as this is not the sociological digression it might at first sight seem: it helps to set the emotional tone of this section of the novel and is not unrelated to the main theme of Ántonia's development. Yet there is much in the description of life in Black Hawk which is not part of this pattern, but of the quite different pattern of the development and career of Jim Burden. These final years at high school before moving on to the University of Nebraska were of course very significant in Jim's career, as they were in that of Miss Cather, who followed a similar progress. Ántonia plays a very minor part in this section, while the gradually maturing Jim looks out in excitement and growing understanding on the social scene in Black Hawk. Is it that Jim is fitting himself to be the ideal observer of Ántonia? That seems to be the only way in which this part of the novel can be structurally justified.

But, as we have noted, the section considered by itself is a remarkable piece of writing. The account of the Harling family, the extraordinary story of Mr. and Mrs. Cutter, scenes at the Boys' Home ("the best hotel on our branch of the Burlington"), the Saturday night dances in the tent set up on the vacant lot, the blind Negro pianist playing at the hotel, and through it all the good-humored and purposeful "hired girls" moving with a freedom and vitality that put the middle-class females of Black Hawk to shame—in this kind of descriptive writing Miss Cather was doing for her part of the country something of what Sarah Orne Jewett had done for New England. There is the flavor of a region and of a community here, and we can see why, in turning to this phase of her story, Willa Cather occasionally lost sight of her main theme. . . .

JIM'S DEPARTURE AND ÁNTONIA'S FALL

In the third section of the novel we lose sight of Ántonia almost completely. This section deals with Jim Burden at the University of Nebraska, his mild affair with Lena Lingard, one of the Swedish farm girls who has come to the city and set up as a dressmaker, and his decision to continue his studies at Harvard. Jim and his development provide the chief center of interest here, and one suspects that Miss Cather is drawing on her own experiences at the University of Nebraska. The high point of this section is an account of a performance of *Camille*, to which Jim takes Lena. The part of Marguerite was taken by a battered old actress, and in many other respects the performance lacked distinction, but for both Jim and Lena this performance of *Camille* by a rather run-down touring company in Lincoln, Nebraska, was one of the great and critical experiences of their lives.

In the fourth section Jim, going home from Harvard in the summer vacation, learns of Ántonia's fate. She had fallen in love with a railroad conductor and gone off to Denver to marry him: but he had not married her, for, unknown to her, he had already lost his job, and he ran off to Mexico leaving her pregnant. Ántonia goes back to her brother's farm subdued but determined to work once again on the land. Jim learns all the details, including the birth of Ántonia's baby, from Mrs. Steavens, who rents the Burdens' old farm. He goes out to see Ántonia and finds her in the fields, shocking wheat: "She was thinner than I had ever seen her, and looked as Mrs. Steavens said, 'worked down,' but there was a new kind of strength in the gravity of her face, and her colour still gave her that look of deep-seated health and ardour. Still? Why, it flashed across me that though so much had happened in her life and in mine, she was barely twenty-four years old."

She tells him that she would always be miserable in a city. "I'd die of lonesomeness. I like to be where I know every stack and tree, and where all the ground is friendly." The Nebraska fields where she and Jim ran about as children now present themselves as the means of her salvation. And yet this rooting of herself in the American soil—a process hastened by her misfortune—is not achieved at the expense of repudiating her European past. They talk of her father. "He's been dead all these years," Ántonia tells Jim, "and yet he is more real to me than almost anybody else. He never goes out of my life. I talk to him and consult him all the time. The older I grow, the better I know him and the more I understand him." This section ends on a note of hope:

As we walked homeward across the fields, the sun dropped and lay like a great golden globe in the low west. While it hung there, the moon rose in the east, as big as a cart-wheel, pale silver and streaked with rose colour, thin as a bubble or a ghost-moon. For five, perhaps ten minutes, the two luminaries confronted each other across the level land, resting on opposite edges of the world.

In that singular light every little tree and shock of wheat, every sunflower stalk and clump of snow-on-the-mountain, drew itself up high and pointed; the very clods and furrows in the fields seemed to stand up sharply. I felt the old pull of the earth, the solemn magic that comes out of those fields at nightfall. I wished I could be a little boy again, and that my way could end there.

Finally, Jim joins the company of Ántonia's friendly ghosts:

"I'll come back," I said earnestly, through the soft, intrusive darkness.

"Perhaps you will"—I felt rather than saw her smile. "But even if you don't, you're here, like my father. So I won't be lonesome."

As I went back alone over that familiar road, I could almost believe that a boy and girl ran along beside me, as our shadows used to do, laughing and whispering to each other in the grass.

Perhaps the book ought to have ended here, with Ántonia left alone in the field in the gathering darkness. The concluding section, which redeems Ántonia to a conventional happy ending, kills altogether that note of implicit tragedy that had been sounded in the earlier part of the novel. Yet the conclusion can be justified: it has an appropriate symbolic quality, and the return to Bohemia implied in Ántonia's marriage to a Bohemian immigrant and raising a family who speak only Czech at home resolves an important aspect of the novel's theme.

ÁNTONIA'S TRIUMPH

The final section takes place twenty years later, when Jim returns to the scenes of his childhood and visits Ántonia. "I heard of her from time to time; that she married, very soon after I last saw her, a young Bohemian, a cousin of Anton Jellinek; that they were poor, and had a large family." When he visits her, surrounded by a large family, he can see at once that she has found her proper function as housewife and mother on a Nebraska farm. . . .

Jim meets Ántonia's husband, a lively, humorous, dependable Czech, a man more fitted by temperament for the gay life of cities than life on a lonely farm.

I could see the little chap, sitting here every evening by the windmill, nursing his pipe and listening to the silence; the wheeze of the pump, the grunting of the pigs, an occasional squawking when the hens were disturbed by a rat. It did rather seem to me that Cuzak had been made the instrument of Ántonia's special mission. This was a fine life, certainly, but it wasn't the kind of life he had wanted to live. I wondered whether the life that was right for one was ever right for two!

Before he leaves, Jim walks out over the familiar countryside:

This was the road over which Ántonia and I came on that night when we got off the train at Black Hawk and were bedded down in the straw, wondering children, being taken we knew not whither. I had only to close my eyes to hear the rumbling of the wagons in the dark, and to be again overcome by that obliterating strangeness. The feelings of that night were so near that I could reach out and touch them with my hand. I had the sense of coming home to myself, and of having found out what a little circle man's experience is. For Ántonia and for me, this had been the road of Destiny; had taken us to those early accidents of fortune which predetermined for us all that we can ever be. Now I understood that the same road was to bring us together again. Whatever we had missed, we possessed together the precious, the incommunicable past.

A FLAWED BUT IMPRESSIVE ACHIEVEMENT

The symbolism seems a little uncertain at the conclusion. The final suggestion that this is the story of Jim and Ántonia and their relations is not really borne out by the story as it has developed. It begins as that, but later the strands separate until we have three main themes all going—the history of Ántonia, the history of Jim, and scenes of Nebraska life. It seems that the autobiographical impulse that redeemed Willa Cather from what she later considered the barren artfulness of *Alexander's Bridge* had its own dangers and was responsible for the abundance of interesting but not wholly dominated material which is to be found in My Ántonia as in *O Pioneers!*. These two novels are in many respects more alike than any other two of her books: both show vitality, liveliness, and a fine descriptive gift; both show a remarkable ability to project characters and incidents as symbols; but in both the variety of material is not fully integrated with the main theme, and autobiography or regional curiosity sometimes leads the story astray. A flawed novel full of life and interest and possessing a powerful emotional rhythm in spite of its imperfect structural pattern is not, however, a mean achievement, and *My Ántonia* will long be read with pleasure and excitement.

Chronology

1873

Wilella Cather (Willa) born on December 7 in Back Creek Valley, Virginia, the eldest child of Charles Cather and Mary Virginia Boak.

1877

Brother Roscoe born.

1880

Brother Douglass born.

1881

Sister Jessica born.

1883

Family moves to Catherton, Nebraska

1884

The Cathers move to Red Cloud, Nebraska, where Willa's father opens a real estate and loan office.

1885–1889

Willa attends school and participates in local theatrical productions; another brother, James, born in 1887; she develops a deep friendship with the Miner family (the inspiration for the Harlings in *My Ántonia*), and meets Annie Sadilek (later Annie Pavelka), the source for Ántonia Shimerda.

1890

Graduates from Red Cloud High School and delivers the commencement speech; that fall, she moves to Lincoln, Nebraska, and takes preparatory classes in order to enroll at the state university.

1891

Now enrolled at the university, Willa publishes an essay on English philosopher Thomas Carlyle in the *Nebraska State Journal*; abandons her ambition of becoming a surgeon and decides to major in the humanities, with an emphasis on the classics.

1892

Publishes her first short story, "Peter."

1893

Begins writing drama reviews and criticism for the *Nebraska State Journal.*

1894

Becomes literary editor of the university annual, *Sombrero.*

1895

Graduates in June and returns to live in Red Cloud; grandmother dies.

1896

Publishes a short story, "On the Divide"; moves to Pittsburgh in June to take the position of editor at the *Home Monthly;* begins writing reviews for the *Pittsburgh Leader.*

1897

After spending the summer in Red Cloud, Willa returns to Pittsburgh and takes a full-time position as editor at the *Pittsburgh Leader.*

1899

Meets and develops an intense friendship with Isabelle McClung, the daughter of a Pittsburgh judge.

1900

Publishes a short story, "Eric Hermannson's Soul," in *Cosmopolitan.*

1901

Moves into the McClung family home; takes a position at Pittsburgh Central High School, teaching Latin and English.

1902

Publishes poems in *Harper's;* spends the summer in Europe with Isabelle McClung.

1903

Publishes her first book, *April Twilights,* a collection of poems; begins teaching English at Allegheny High School, a position she will hold until 1906.

1905

Publishes a short-story collection, *The Troll Garden*, which includes "Paul's Case," one of her finest stories.

1906

Moves to New York in May to join *McClure's Magazine* as managing editor, a position she will hold for five years.

1908

Meets New England regionalist writer Sarah Orne Jewett, who will have a profound influence on her fiction; moves into an apartment with fellow Nebraskan Edith Lewis, and they will continue to live together until Cather's death in 1947.

1909

Writes *The Life of Mary Baker Eddy and the History of Christian Science*, but it is published as being written by Georgine Milmine; travels to London and meets literary greats H.G. Wells and Ford Madox Ford.

1910

Meets Elizabeth Shepley Sergeant, who will later write an important memoir of her friendship with Willa Cather.

1911

Travels again to England for *McClure's*, and then takes a leave of absence to spend the fall with Isabelle McClung; completes her first novel, *Alexander's Bridge*, and writes "Alexandra," which will later form part of her novel *O Pioneers!*

1912

After magazine serialization, *Alexander's Bridge* is published in April by Houghton Mifflin; Cather makes an important trip to the Southwest, where she decides to dedicate herself completely to writing fiction.

1913

Publishes *O Pioneers!* in June; meets and becomes friends with opera singer Olive Fremstad, who serves as the model for Thea Kronberg, the central character in her next novel, *The Song of the Lark*.

1914

Ghost writes S.S. McClure's *My Autobiography*.

1915

The Song of the Lark is published in October.

1916

Cather is traumatized by the marriage of Isabelle McClung to violinist Jan Hambourg; she travels widely throughout the Southwest, Wyoming, and Nebraska; renews her friendship with Annie Pavelka.

1917

Spends the summer in Jaffrey, New Hampshire, which will become her favorite place to write; works on *My Ántonia*.

1918

My Ántonia is published in October.

1920

Cather leaves Houghton Mifflin and begins her long association with the publishing house of Alfred Knopf; in September, Knopf publishes a short-story collection, *Youth and the Bright Medusa*.

1922

Publishes *One of Ours*, a novel of World War I.

1923

One of Ours is awarded the Pulitzer Prize; *A Lost Lady* published in September.

1924–1925

Visits novelist D.H. Lawrence in New Mexico; while there, she comes across Rev. William Howlett's biography of Father Joseph Marchbeuf, who will serve as the inspiration for Father Joseph in *Death Comes for the Archbishop; The Professor's House* is published in September 1925.

1926

Spends the summer in New Mexico; *My Mortal Enemy* is published in October.

1927

Death Comes for the Archbishop published in September.

1928

Father dies in March, and later that year Cather's mother suffers a serious stroke; travels to Quebec and begins writing *Shadows on the Rock*.

1929

Elected to the National Institute of Arts and Letters.

1930

Awarded the Howells medal of American Academy of Arts and Letters for *Death Comes for the Archbishop.*

1931

Shadows on the Rock published in August; Cather's mother dies; visits Red Cloud for the last time.

1932

Publishes *Obscure Destinies,* a collection of three novellas, one of which, "Neighbor Rosicky," draws again on the Pavelka family.

1933

Awarded Prix Femina Americain for *Shadows on the Rock.*

1935

Lucy Gayheart published in August; travels to Italy with Edith Lewis.

1936

Knopf publishes a collection of Cather's essays, *Not Under Forty.*

1938

Visits her mother's birthplace in Virginia to gather material for her final novel, *Sapphira and the Slave Girl;* brother Douglass dies in June, and Isabelle McClung dies in October.

1940

Sapphira and the Slave Girl is published in December.

1944

Awarded the National Institute of Arts and Letters Gold Medal for fiction.

1945

Completes her last story, "The Best Years"; brother Roscoe dies.

1947

Dies in New York of a massive cerebral hemorrhage on April 24; is buried in Jaffrey, New Hampshire.

FOR FURTHER RESEARCH

CRITICISM

Edward A. and Lillian D. Bloom, *Willa Cather's Gift of Sympathy*. Carbondale: Southern Illinois University Press, 1962.

L. Brent Bohlke, ed., *Willa Cather in Person: Interviews, Speeches, Letters*. Lincoln: University of Nebraska Press, 1986.

David Daiches, *Willa Cather: A Critical Introduction*. Ithaca, NY: Cornell University Press, 1951.

Maxwell Geismar, *The Last of the Provincials*. Boston: Houghton Mifflin, 1947.

Philip Gerber, *Willa Cather*. Boston: Twayne, 1975.

Hermione Lee, *Willa Cather: Double Lives*. New York: Pantheon, 1989.

Dorothy Tuck McFarland, *Willa Cather*. New York: Frederick Unger, 1972.

Jo Ann Middleton, *Willa Cather's Modernism*. Rutherford, NJ: Farleigh Dickinson University Press, 1990.

John J. Murphey, ed., *Critical Essays on Willa Cather*. Boston: G.K. Hall, 1984.

——, *My Ántonia: The Road Home*. Boston: Twayne, 1989.

Sharon O'Brien, *Willa Cather: The Emerging Voice*. New York: Oxford University Press, 1987.

John H. Randall III, *The Landscape and the Looking Glass: Willa Cather's Search for Value*. Boston: Houghton Mifflin, 1960.

Susan J. Rosowski, *The Voyage Perilous: Willa Cather's Romanticism*. Lincoln: University of Nebraska Press, 1986.

——, ed., *Approaches to Teaching Cather's "My Ántonia."* New York: Modern Language Association, 1989.

Mary Ryder, *Willa Cather and Classical Myth: The Search for a New Parnassus*. Lewistown, NY: Edwin Mellen Press, 1990.

James Schroeter, ed., *Willa Cather and Her Critics*. Ithaca, NY: Cornell University Press, 1967.

David Stouck, *Willa Cather's Imagination*. Lincoln: University of Nebraska Press, 1975.

Dorothy Van Ghent, *Willa Cather.* Minneapolis: University of Minnesota Press, 1964.

BIOGRAPHICAL AND HISTORICAL WORKS OF INTEREST

Marilyn Arnold, *Willa Cather: A Reference Guide.* Boston: G.K. Hall, 1986.

Mildred R. Bennett, *The World of Willa Cather.* Lincoln: University of Nebraska Press, 1961.

E.K. Brown and Leon Edel, *Willa Cather: A Critical Biography.* New York: Knopf, 1953.

Robert L. Heilbroner and Aaron Singer, *The Economic Transformation of America: 1600 to the Present.* Fort Worth: Harcourt Brace College, 1999.

Edith Lewis, *Willa Cather Living.* New York: Knopf, 1953.

Elizabeth Shepley Sergeant, *Willa Cather: A Memoir.* Philadelphia: J.B. Lippincourt, 1953.

James Woodress, *Willa Cather: A Literary Life.* Lincoln: University of Nebraska Press, 1987.

WORKS BY WILLA CATHER

April Twilights. Boston: R.G. Badger, 1903. Rev. ed. New York: Knopf, 1923.

The Troll Garden. New York: McClure, Philips, 1905.

The Life of Mary Baker G. Eddy and the History of Christian Science. New York: Doubleday, 1909. Ostensibly by Georgina Milnine, but actually written by Willa Cather.

Alexander's Bridge. Boston: Houghton Mifflin, 1912.

O Pioneers! Boston: Houghton Mifflin, 1913.

My Autobiography. New York: Frederick A. Stokes, 1914. Ostensibly by S.S. McClure, but actually written by Willa Cather.

The Song of the Lark. Boston: Houghton Mifflin, 1915.

My Ántonia. Boston: Houghton Mifflin, 1918.

Youth and the Bright Medusa. New York: Knopf, 1920.

One of Ours. New York: Knopf, 1922.

A Lost Lady. New York: Knopf, 1923.

The Professor's House. New York: Knopf, 1925.

My Mortal Enemy. New York: Knopf, 1926.

Death Comes for the Archbishop. New York: Knopf, 1927.

Shadows on the Rock. New York: Knopf, 1931.

Obscure Destinies. New York: Knopf, 1932.

Lucy Gayheart. New York: Knopf, 1935.

Not Under Forty. New York: Knopf, 1936.

Sapphira and the Slave Girl. New York: Knopf, 1940.

INDEX

on her orchards, 60
as a "hired girl," 43, 65
importance of past for,
113
impressionistic portrayal
of, 162, 164–67
independence from men,
121
influence of Peter/Pavel
wolf story on, 108–109
innocence in, 113–14
life cycle represented in,
81–82
looking toward the future,
115, 116
as a "mine of life," 133
modeled after real person,
64
as most heroic of Cather's
characters, 54–55
narrative insufficiently
portraying, 146
and Nebraska country
adapting to, 74
bond with, 141–42, 188
parallels with, 135,
136–41
preferring over city,
114–15
as objectification of
narrator's emotions, 182
paths with Jim, 128–29
diverging, 130–31
parallel, 128–29
physical contrasts with
Lena, 168
preserving wild and free
spirit, 142, 143
rebuilding life, 46
representing vitality of
life, 11–12
sexuality in, 70, 71, 92–93,
97
shaping her personal

destiny, 153–54
shared experiences with
Jim, 106–107
storytelling by, 109
symbolism of, 79
triumphing over
adversity, 75
unconditional love by, 120
as woman wronged,
82–83
see also characters, Jim
Burden
Anton Jelinek, 38, 159
Blind d'Arnault (piano
player), 156–57
Burden family 37
Ántonia criticizing
grandfather, 137
grandmother contrasted
with Ántonia, 96
Jim's forced image of,
174–75
Mrs. Burden, 89
religion of, 72
and Shimerda family, 42,
183
drawn from real life, 51,
52–53, 60
Gaston Cleric, 37, 44, 85,
101, 154
Harling family, 38, 65, 92
Frances, 74
Mr. Harling, 157
Mrs. Harling, 165
Nina, 110
hired girls
community among, 158
compared with other
townspeople, 147–48,
186–87
innocence in, 113–14
and Jim Burden
favoring, 92, 114
picnic with, 98–100